The Air Force Role in Developing International Outer Space Law

DELBERT R. TERRILL JR., Colonel, USAFR

Air Force History and Museums Program

Air University Press
Maxwell Air Force Base, Alabama

May 1990

Disclaimer

Opinions, conclusions, and recommendations expressed or implied within are solely those of the author and do not necessary represent the views of Air University, the United States Air Force, the Department of Defense, or any other US government agency. Cleared for public release, distribution.

Digitize January 2003 from May 1999 Printing NOTE: Pagination changed.

For USAFA '70

Contents

Foreword

The impact of the US defense and space initiatives on bilateral and multilateral treaties and on international outer space law in general, a topic of much current discussion, is better understood by an analysis of the development of that body of law. Col Delbert "Chip" Terrill Jr. discusses its early evolution and the Air Force contribution to it. He describes the Air Force's ad hoc approach to international outer space law and its efforts to have this approach adopted by the United States and the international community.

Further, the author details the profound impact that the surprise attack at Pearl Harbor on 7 December 1941 had on President Dwight D. Eisenhower. He vowed never again to allow the US to be similarly vulnerable to a surprise attack, particularly in a nuclear environment. As part of his efforts to preclude a surprise attack on the United States, Eisenhower sought to establish the concept of free passage of intelligence gathering satellites as part of accepted international outer space law. The author traces how the Eisenhower administration demonstrated a lack of concern about being first in space so long as the concept of free passage in outer space was universally accepted. However, the administration apparently and clearly underestimated the propaganda value that being first would have. Colonel Terrill traces how the Eisenhower administration failed to fully communicate its policy goal of achieving such free passage to the uniformed services. Although civilian leaders in the Defense Department were aware of the administration's position, the Air Force and the other military services at times acted at cross purposes to the concept of free passage.

Chip Terrill describes the Air Force's continued efforts to resist the passage of most international outer space law conventions, the restiveness of the Air Force judge advocate general (JAG) corps with a backseat role, and how the JAG generally failed in its early attempt to have the Air Force become proactive in the development of the law. Ironically, Terrill illustrates how the Air Force's ad hoc approach essentially dovetailed with Eisenhower's goal of free passage. Colonel Terrill relates how the Air Force's Project West

Ford caused the passage of certain environmentally sensitive provisions of international outer space law.

The author closes by examining the comment and coordination process leading to the passage of the Liability for Damages Convention.* Such was typical of the Air Force's lukewarm, reactive posture regarding the passage of international conventions, except for the Agreement on Rescue and Return of Astronauts, † which the Air Force strongly supported.

In short, this superb work documents the interesting gestation period regarding the development of international outer space law. It will undoubtedly contribute to the development of Air Force doctrine by providing a better understanding of the Air Force's involvement in the development of international outer space law.

Jacob Neufeld, Senior Historian
Air Force History Support Office

---

* Convention on the International Liability for Damage Caused by Space Objects.
† Agreement on the Rescue of Astronauts, the Return of Astronauts and the Return of Objects Launched into Space About the Return of Objects Launched into Space

About the Author

Delbert R. "Chip" Terrill Jr. is an administrative law judge with the United States Federal Energy Regulatory Commission. Judge Terrill is a colonel in the USAF Reserves and serves as a historian with the Air Force Historical Research Agency, Maxwell Air Force Base (AFB), Alabama. He received a BS degree (majoring in history) from the United States Air Force Academy in 1970 and a JD degree in 1974 from the Georgetown University Law Center. Judge Terrill has worked at the White House and on Capitol Hill, and with the Office of US Special Counsel. He has served as a special assistant US attorney and as a department counsel and hearing examiner (now administrative judge) with the Department of Defense (DOD) Legal Services Agency's Directorate for Industrial Security Clearance Review (now Office of Hearings and Appeals). While in the Air Force Reserve, he previously served at the Department of Legal Medicine, Armed Forces Institute of Pathology, and the Office of the Surgeon General of the Air Force. He is a graduate of the Air War College (outstanding graduate), the Armed Forces Staff College, and the Air Force Squadron Officer School. In February 1994 and July 1997, Colonel Terrill attended the Sixth and Seventh Biennial Conferences on the Law Relating to National Security Activities in Outer Space. His prior publications include "Complaint Procedures Initiated by and Against Federal Administrative Law Judges Need Reform Now," Judge's Journal (Fall 1994); Chapter Two "The Patient, the Hospital and the Law," Lawyers Medical Cyclopedia (Allan Smith Publishing Company, 1981); and "The New Copyright Law: How It Affects Physicians," The Journal of Legal Medicine (1977).

Acknowledgment

I would like to thank the individuals who assisted me in the research and preparation of this monograph. Will H. Carroll, Prof Harry H. Almond Jr., and Brig Gen Martin Menter, USAF, Retired, all provided invaluable interviews and documents. Robbie Profitt of the Federal Aviation Administration assisted me in locating crucial Air Coordinating Committee papers. Mrs. Albert M. Kuhfeld provided me access to her husband's files. Eilene Galloway allowed me to pick her brain periodically. R. Cargill Hall provided me early access to his insightful works analyzing the origins of US space policy, which explain in detail the Eisenhower administration's thinking and efforts to assure acceptance of its "freedom of space" policy. The officials of the Air Force Historical Research Agency, Maxwell Air Force Base, Alabama, graciously allowed me the flexibility of completing this long-term project as a part of my agency duties. The librarians at the National Academy of Sciences and the archivists at the National Records Center and the National Archives and Records Administration were always helpful and pleasant. Most importantly, thanks are due to Jacob Neufeld, who guided the direction of my research and my writing and whose welcomed red pen was always ready and on the money, and to Thomas C. Lobenstein and Peggy Smith, my Air University Press editors, for their willingness to put up with my last-minute additions and changes. Thanks also to Karen Fleming-Michael for reading, copyediting, and logistic support. Finally, thanks to James Howard and Richard Wolf who prevented the succeeding generations of computer software programs from disorganizing the iterations of this monograph and who thereby kept me sane.

Introduction

In this monograph the author describes the United States Air Force resistance to the passage of international conventions (treaties) and the general impact that Air Force opposition had on the development of international law regarding outer space. International outer space law, like other international law, is created by court decisions (international and domestic), passage (negotiation and ratification) of international treaties or conventions, and commonly accepted practices of nations, which in turn become customs. In addition, the publications by scholars of international outer space law have had a substantial impact on the evolution of this body of law.

Even before space activities had actually begun, academics and jurists pushed for the early passage of certain conventions governing the use of space. The US government, encouraged in large part by the Air Force, chose to delay action until space operations had begun so that these actual activities themselves and the commonly accepted customs derived from them, rather than the theory of jurists, would drive the development of space law. The focus here is on the Air Force's role in the evolution of outer space law primarily from the mid-1950s to the early 1960s. The author then examines Air Force efforts to preclude an international agreement (treaty) defining sovereignty in outer space similar to the convention[*] (known as the Chicago Convention) defining national airspace that was agreed to at the 1944 meetings of the International Civil Aviation Organization (ICAO) in Chicago. Sovereignty and the delimitation of where airspace ends and outer space begins have been inextricably tied.

Over the years, these two issues have generated much of the debate on outer space law. The first substantive treatise (published in 1951) urged that the development of outer space law focus on the sovereignty issue. Subsequently, authors of numerous articles and proposals sought to establish a clear line of demarcation between outer space and airspace. While military personnel in operational forces may have a gut feeling as to what is outer space,

---

[*] Convention on International Civil Aviation

neither international conventions nor customarily accepted practices have established a commonly accepted line of demarcation between these two regions. Although the debate continues about where airspace ends and outer space begins, the issue of whether or not sovereignty may be asserted in outer space has been generally settled by customary practice. There is freedom of passage in outer space and, accordingly, no state may claim sovereignty over outer space. [1]

In response to the early efforts by theorists and academicians to conclude an international outer space convention, the Air Force proposed-and the United States adopted-an ad hoc approach to the creation of international outer space law, reasoning that this approach would allow practice and technology to drive the evolution of the law. Given that the president's Air Coordinating Committee (ACC) had authority to establish the US position to be presented to the International Civil Aviation Organization (ICAO), the Air Force, as an ACC member, encouraged and obtained the ACC's adoption of the Air Force position. Accordingly, during sessions of the ICAO, the US opposed several efforts to conclude a convention regarding outer space. [2] The ICAO generally adopted the US position.

Having set this approach in motion during the 1950s, the Air Force, in the following decade, did not playa major role in the development of international outer space law-much to the chagrin of certain members of the Air Force judge advocate general (JAG) corps. While Air Force lawyers had initially encouraged the ad hoc approach, by 1961 the judge advocate general himself expressed discomfort with the reactive posture undertaken by the Air Force. Consequently, he recommended that the Air Force seize the leadership and take a more active role in the development of outer space law, as the Air Force had done in the field of aerospace medicine. The Air Force never followed this advice. It instead remained in the reactive mode; when tasked to do so, the Air Force coordinated and commented on the various international conventions of outer space law being considered. [3] The only other exception to the Air Force's passive role in the development of the law was an unintended impact resulting from Project West Ford. Because of this project, certain environmental protection provisions were included as part of the 1968 Principles Treaty* (see chapter 4).

The Air Force's reactive posture to proposed international conventions was typified by its involvement in the internal US government negotiations leading to the passage of the 1972 Convention on International Liability for Damages Caused by Space Objects. Because of this approach, the Air Force is not perceived as having the legal expertise or reputation in outer space law that it has developed, for example, in the area of aerospace medicine. [4] To capture the nature of this reactive posture, the author describes the Air Force's participation in these generally internal DOD negotiations in minute detail. No direct evidence indicates that the Air Force's reactive approach impaired its missions, doctrine, or interests.

The assessment of the US role in the evolution of international outer space law involves an analysis of the US policy formulation process. Determining what if any institutional reputation the Air Force may have lost by not being more active in influencing this policy process or by not being viewed as the US "legal expert" in international outer space law would only be speculative. To determine what, if any, leverage or influence the Air Force has lost would require a more in-depth study of the Air Force's role in national policy formulation and is beyond the scope of this monograph.

When and where the Air Force outwardly has influenced the development of international outer space law, such involvement has been, predominantly, a result of the efforts of the attorneys assigned to the Air Force Office of General Counsel (OGC) and JAG offices. This monograph does not catalogue the many articles and presentations written or made by these Air Force officials. While such articles and presentations may have influenced the evolution of the law, their impact would be difficult to assess. Instead, this monograph traces the interaction of Air Force officials with the various policy-making levels of government inside and outside DOD during the consideration of proposed international

---

* Treaty on the Principles Governing Activities in the Exploration and Use of Outer Space, Including the Moon and Other Celestial Bodies

conventions affecting outer space. With the exception of its JAG corps and OGC attorneys, the Air Force has not been particularly active in attempting to influence the development of outer space law. This passivity may be due, in part, to the fact that the impact of other parts of the Air Force on this body of international law is difficult to determine because, generally outside of JAG and OGC, in the 1950s and 1960s Air Force organizations did not carefully document their roles and positions on space law issues.

On the other hand, it must be understood that international outer space law generally evolved from the practice of nations and that the operational forces of the Air Force were and remain the leading US military service impacting outer space matters. [5] When this monograph discusses US military practices regarding outer space, it generally refers to Air Force operational practices. Accordingly, the operational forces of the Air Force established, through their practices rather than by formal statement of their positions, the customs that in turn developed the law.

------

[1] In 1976, Columbia, the Congo, Ecuador, Indonesia, Kenya, Uganda, and Zaire declared that a geostationary orbit 22,300 miles above earth was part of the sovereign territory of the state under which the orbit lies. The United States, among others, opposed their declaration of sovereignty. The position of this Bogota Declaration has yet to become accepted international law by convention, custom, or practice. Nevertheless, the principle espoused by the declaration is still being debated. See Declaration of Bogota, 3 December 1976, text found in Journal of Space Law (1978), 169.

[2] As an exception to this general rule, the Air Force strongly supported passage of the convention regarding rescue and return of astronauts (see chapter 6 below).

[3] By the early 1980s, the Air Force general counsel and JAG began sponsoring the biennial Conference on the Law Relating to National Security Activities in Outer Space. Sponsorship of these conferences over the past 16 years has reflected a subtle change in the Air Force's posture.

[4] Perhaps, the Air Force reputation and expertise in outer space law is increasing as a result of its sponsorship of the biennial conference regarding national security and the law of outer space.

[5] DOD Directive 5160.32, Development of Space Systems, promulgated by Secretary of Defense Robert S. McNamara on 6 March 1961, established the Air Force as DOD's executive agent for space matters. This directive was intended to overcome fragmentation of effort, avoid duplication, and increase efficiency.

Chapter 1

Germination of Outer Space as a Legal Concept

The Paris and Chicago Conventions of 1919 and 1944,[*] respectively, recognized the exclusive sovereignty of states to the airspace above their territory. Delegates did not discuss outer space as such. Thus they established no line of demarcation as to where airspace ended and outer space began. Whether national sovereignty extended indefinitely over a nation's territory was not resolved. [1]

Even with the rapid changes in technology extending flight higher and higher, sovereignty over outer space was seldom discussed until the early 1950s. By then the launching of rockets into space and plans to boost an object into orbit made discussion of this issue more imperative. As has often occurred, not until technology demands does a development in or of the law follow. From the beginning, the sovereignty issue-how high a state's sovereignty extends, if at all, into outer space-has been the genesis of much discussion regarding outer space law. While many other outer space law issues were eventually resolved, the issue of how high sovereignty extends-the issue that started much of the discussion-remains unresolved.

In 1951 John Cobb Cooper-law professor and head of the Institute of Air and Space Law, McGill University in Montreal, and a member of the Princeton University Institute for Advanced Study-published "High Altitude Flight and National Sovereignty," a seminal and thought-provoking treatise. [2] Professor Cooper had served as part of the US delegation to the 1944 ICAO meetings and was a major force behind the decision to conclude the Chicago Convention. His 1951 treatise generated substantial discussion within the legal and scientific communities regarding the need to define where airspace became outer space. [3]

---

[*] International Convention for Air Navigation and Convention on International Civil Aviation. respectively

Professor John Cobb Cooper and first graduating class from McGill University's Institute of Air and Space Law. From left to right: David Upsher (Canada), unidentified, Ming-Min Peng (Taiwan), Ishmael Abdulmonein (Egypt, partially obscured behind Peng), Ian McPherson (Canada), Jean Nemeth (Hungary), Dean Meredith (dean of McGill's Law School), Hamilton DeSaussure (United States), Dr. Cooper, Constantine Vaicoussis (Greece), Dr. Julian Gazdik (Poland, Institute's associate director), John Fenston (Canada), and Niky Hesse (Germany).

Cooper's article led to a clamor by academics and international jurists for a definition of outer space. Their efforts to achieve a clear delimitation between airspace and outer space were driven by the hope that outer space might be "saved from the chaos of national rivalries." [4] They theorized that once outer space was defined by international" agreement, all claims regarding it would be easily resolved. These scholars and jurists likewise theorized that freedom of exploration in outer space would evolve similarly to the exploration of the sea. Otherwise, it was feared that the "outcome of the growing interest in outer space [would] result in a constantly increasing clash of interest between those states most interested in outer space, and between [their] citizens." [5] Prince Welf Heinrich of Hanover of the Gesellschaft für Weltraumforschung [6] (the [German] Society for Space Flight) noted that nations did not have the same needs and interests in outer space as they had in airspace. He further noted that nations could not control (police) outer space even if they declared outer space as being part of their sovereignty. Thus, he argued that sovereignty should not extend into outer space.* Prince Heinrich argued that a resolution of the boundary between airspace and outer space was, however, needed to assure the freedom of exploration in outer space. [7] If they did not resolve the sovereignty issue, nations would likely make territorial claims based on the landing of scientific devices on bodies in outer space. [8]

Eisenhower, a Nuclear Pearl Harbor, and Air Force Balloons

Prior to Professor Cooper's treatise, many elements within the United States, including the US Army Air Forces (AAF), had been interested in outer space and its potential exploitation for military or intelligence purposes. Concurrent with Project RAND's start up in 1946, Maj Gen Curtis E. LeMay, deputy chief of staff for research and development, directed that RAND assist the AAF in demonstrating its capabilities vis-à-vis space. Within three weeks, RAND produced a study titled Preliminary Design of an Experimental World-Circling Spaceship, an engineering analysis of satellite feasibility. This 1946 study concluded that such satellites were an unlikely base for offensive weapons. [9]

By April 1951, Project RAND had completed an Air Force sponsored study contemplating the eventuality of earth observation satellites. As a result of the RAND report and because the Air Force Strategic Air Command needed assistance in developing reconnaissance that could help determine appropriate targets behind the Iron Curtain, the Air Force, in January 1952, convened a Beacon Hill study group (formally titled Project Lincoln) under the auspices of the Massachusetts Institute of Technology (MIT). [10] The study group was to assess various issues generated by such satellites. The study group included industry scientists and academicians. [11] In its final report issued in June 1952, the Beacon Hill group concluded that observation satellite systems could infringe on another country's sovereignty. Its report specifically acknowledged the potential for "intrusion" over Soviet territory. [12]

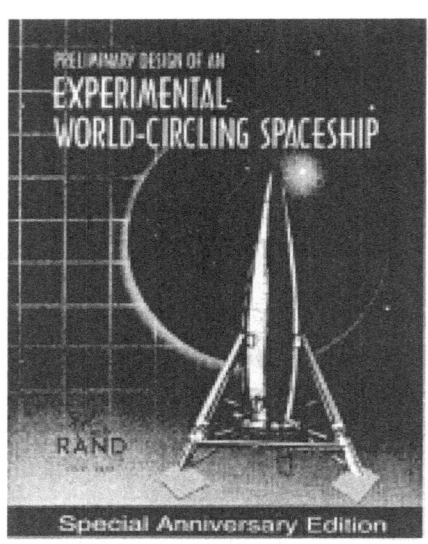

Cover of Preliminary design of an
Experimental World-Circling Spaceship

On 24 February and 27 March 1954, President Dwight D. Eisenhower met with his National Security Council (NSC) and then with the civilian scientists of the Science Advisory Committee in the Office of Defense Mobilization. With the memory of Pearl Harbor still fresh in his mind, Eisenhower related his concern regarding the potential for a surprise nuclear attack on the United States. [13] Stressing the need for avoiding or containing such aggression, President Eisenhower was resolved to ensure that the United States would never again be vulnerable to a direct sneak attack. [14] He challenged the US scientific community to address his concern. In response, scientists created the Surprise Attack Panel-later known as the Technological Capabilities Panel (TCP)-chaired by MIT president James R. Killian. [15] The panel issued its final report, "Meeting the Threat of Surprise Attack," on 14 February 1955. Among other things, the report recommended that the United States develop satellites to operate at high altitudes. These satellites would establish as a principle of international law the freedom of passage for any subsequent military satellites. [16] The panel had created a blueprint for Eisenhower as to how the US should proceed regarding resolution of the freedom of passage issue.

Given a lack of intelligence regarding the Union of Soviet Socialist Republics (USSR) and given that the United States was not able to implement the reconnaissance satellite system envisioned by the TCP,

President Eisenhower initiated Project Genetrix in January 1956. This space "research" project consisted of the Air Force launching 516 Skyhook "weather" balloons from locations in Europe. [17] These balloons carried automatic cameras. Given prevailing winds, the balloons were certain to pass over Eastern Europe and the USSR. If the research succeeded, the balloons-equipped with radio tracking beacons-were eventually to be recovered near Japan and Alaska. The program produced limited intelligence. [18]

When the balloons passed over their territory, Eastern European nations and the USSR protested, complaining that the balloons disrupted civilian aircraft and were equipped for automatic aerial photography in an effort to obtain targeting information. Belgium and Czechoslovakian airlines canceled several flights to Czechoslovakia because of the balloons. The United States initially admitted that Radio Free Europe, an affiliate of a "privately financed anticommunist organization in the US," was flying propaganda balloons from West Germany. Further, the Air Force admitted that as part of Operation Moby Dick, it had released some two thousand balloons from various sites around the earth but denied that these releases were a threat to civilian flights. [19]

On 7 February 1956, Secretary of State John Foster Dulles responded to the Soviet protests by stating that, in the interest of "decent friendly relations," the US would "try" to stop the release of the "weather" balloons. While admitting that some of the weather balloons carried photographic equipment, the United States asserted that the equipment was only for taking pictures of high-altitude cloud formations. [20] The Soviets responded that they had developed film from the balloons containing pictures of Turkish airfields. [21] In the face of criticism that the balloons clearly violated the USSR's airspace, Dulles agreed to stop releasing them. He noted, however, that "the ownership of upper air" was "a disputable question under international law." [22] Some in the media attacked Dulles for making this statement and for having approved the launch of the balloons.

These critics argued that the sovereignty issue had long been resolved and that sovereignty extended indefinitely into the sky. Further, they argued that the Chicago Convention forbade the sending of unmanned missiles over another nation's airspace without consent. The position of these critics was correct with respect to a nation's sovereign rights over its own airspace. However, no international law, practice, or custom had as yet established the issue of a nation's sovereignty in outer space.

Further, the position of these critics was diametrically opposed to Eisenhower's goal of achieving freedom of passage for intelligence gathering satellites in outer space as had been initially envisioned by the Surprise Attack Panel.

After Dulles' response, the Air Force disputed that its balloons were intended for anything other than charting the jet stream. [23] The Air Force cover story stating that the balloons "were being used for weather research also made reference to the International Geophysical Year (IGY)." [24] When the Air Force later proposed to release even higher flying balloons in mid-March 1956, Eisenhower informed Gen Nathan F. Twining, Air Force chief of staff, that he (Eisenhower) "was not interested in any more balloons" and terminated any further launches. [25]

In the meantime, a more promising avenue of gathering information, the U-2, was becoming operational and would make its maiden flight five months after Eisenhower ordered an end to the balloon flights. [26] By 1956 the practices of the Air Force and others involved in the balloon "experiments" and the contemplation of an earth orbiting observation system had focused substantial attention on and begun a dialogue regarding international outer space law.

"Space-far-Peace" and the International Geophysical Year

Driven by the advent of IGY-1 July 1957-31 December 1958-and other considerations, the United States and the USSR increased their focus on their respective space programs. [27] On 15 April 1955 the USSR announced the establishment of its Special Commission for Interplanetary Communications, making reference to a globe circling satellite program. [28] In 1955 the US was completing the formulation of its first space policy, but it did so in a somewhat ambivalent manner. The United States assumed that its space program was technologically superior to the USSR's space program. Indeed, the US was far ahead of the Soviets in miniaturizing its warhead devices (which fact was highly classified at that time); however, as discussed later, this US advantage was to become a double-edged sword.

President Dwight D. Eisenhower, Gen Nathan F. Twining, and Secretary of State John Foster Dulles

In drafting its space policy, the Eisenhower administration demonstrated an ambivalent desire to be first in space. Such ambivalence by Eisenhower was not unique to outer space but was generally the hallmark of Eisenhower's approach to problem solving, particularly and ironically regarding issues relating to foreign affairs. [29] For example, Eisenhower pursued a space-for-peace policy and proposed to rely upon nonexistent "nonmilitary" boosters as the launch vehicle. As drafted by Air Force secretary Donald A. Quarles,* this policy declared that the IGY satellite program would not interfere with intercontinental and intermediate range ballistic missile (ICBM and IRBM) programs. The US satellite would be launched for "peaceful purposes" and would assist in establishing the right of unimpeded overflights in outer space. [30] This decision was confirmed by the National Security Council (NSC Directive 5520, Draft Statement of Policy on US Scientific Satellite Program) on 26 May and approved by President Eisenhower on 27 May 1955. However, the administration did not immediately communicate this decision to the military services, [31] one of which was to be assigned to manage the development of the boosters. [32]

By pursuing a space-for-peace policy, President Eisenhower, at least publicly, began a persistent effort by his administration to marry space

7

exploration, disarmament, and the creation of international law, providing that space was free from national military rivalries. [33] As noted earlier, underlying Eisenhower's space-for-peace policy was his resolve to prevent a nuclear Pearl Harbor. Following the blueprint provided by the Surprise Attack Panel, he sought to obtain a free passage for intelligence-gathering satellites in outer space as being essential to preventing a surprise attack. Therefore, while publicly articulating a space-for-peace policy, Eisenhower maneuvered to obtain freedom of passage for intelligence-gathering devices in outer space. [34] He saw no inconsistency in his stalking-horse strategy.

While the product of such intelligence-gathering satellites could clearly be used to facilitate warfare by identifying targets, Eisenhower perceived that the satellites were passive not "offensive" and argued that it was his intent that they be used to maintain peace. As part of his "open skies" proposal, Eisenhower offered to share such intelligence with the Soviets much the same as President Ronald W. Reagan would propose 30 years later. Eisenhower hoped that the free passage of IGY scientific satellites in outer space would establish the precedent of free passage for subsequent intelligence-gathering satellites. [35] Accordingly, the Eisenhower administration worked to ensure that an earth satellite project was included as part of the US IGY program. [36]

While maneuvering to include a scientific satellite system as part of IGY. President Eisenhower waited until the Geneva summit with Soviet premier Nikita Khrushchev in July 1955 to propose the US open skies position. [37] Eisenhower suggested that as part of open skies the United States and USSR provide facilities from which aerial photography taken of the other could be shared, thereby precluding any surprise attack. The USSR rejected the open skies proposal as a ploy for gathering target data. [38] The USSR stuck to its claim of absolute sovereignty of all its space (air and outer) over its homeland. [39]

Upon returning to the United States from Geneva, President Eisenhower announced officially on 29 July 1955 that the here-to-fore undisclosed US IGY satellite project was to be powered by nonmilitary boosters that had not yet been built. [40] In September 1955 the Navy's proposal to manage the "civilian" IGY booster program was approved. Neither President Eisenhower nor his advisers appear to have appreciated how much their idealistic insistence on developing nonmilitary boosters would delay the American satellite project and what the impact of that delay would be. [41] No IGY boosters were ever fully developed and launched under the Navy's Viking-AerobeeHi/Vanguard program. [42] However, the military services did not cease working on their boosters and continued to attempt to launch them. [43] When the Navy's Vanguard program ebbed, the secretary of defense turned too late to the Air Force in hopes of launching a satellite during the IGY program. [44]

Who Would Be First in Space?

Some have concluded that the USSR was first in space by default because of Eisenhower's "ambivalence" and his secretary of defense's penchant for fiscal conservatism regarding space programs. [45] These factors might partially explain why the United States failed to be first in space. Other factors explain why the USSR was first in space with Sputnik.* First, Eisenhower had been assured that physics precluded dropping a bomb from a satellite in orbit; therefore, he was not concerned about a surprise attack from outer space. Second, the Eisenhower administration did not fully appreciate the "psychological shock value" of a successful Sputnik launch or the reaction of the American people to having Sputnik overhead. [46] Third, Eisenhower's administration did not appreciate fully the propaganda and prestige value of being "first in space," [47] despite warnings to this effect by the National Security Council, the scientific community's TCP, and RAND. Finally, and probably most importantly, the US was not first in space because the US held a significant lead over the USSR in miniaturizing its hydrogen bomb devices.

Secretary of Defense
Charles E. Wilson

9

While Eisenhower was concerned about a nuclear surprise attack, the main emphasis of the US missile program (including budgetary spending) was not the launching of a satellite into space but the precise delivery of a hydrogen warhead anywhere on earth. Because of its miniaturization advantage, the United States did not need rockets with heavy throw weights (thrust). In fact, in the years before Sputnik, the Air Force had actually reduced the number of stages in its Atlas program. Because the USSR warhead devices were larger and heavier, they required the concomitant development of rockets with greater thrust than did the US devices. While the United States was ahead in being able to deliver a hydrogen warhead more precisely anywhere on earth, the USSR had rockets with greater thrust and throw weights that were advantageous for launching objects into outer space. The US focus on attaining a technological/miniaturization advantage was disadvantageous to its being first in space. [48]

Secretary of the Air Force
Donald A. Quarles

Given the underestimation of the "shock effect" of Sputnik, given the perception that we were technologically far ahead of the USSR in space, and given Eisenhower's interest in establishing the principle of freedom of passage for spy satellites, the failure to push such a crash program is understandable. Nonetheless, it was probable that the US could have been first in space had the president established that achievement as a national goal. [49] As an example of his administration's commitment to ensuring the principle of free passage in outer space, the Eisenhower administration (Quarles) in 1956 "restrained" government officials from

10

any public discussion of spaceflight. [50] Eisenhower administration officials feared that any discussion of military space operations would engender a "worldwide debate" on outer space law issues. They further feared that the debate might result in efforts to preclude the passage in outer space of military related devices. [51]

Despite Eisenhower's "civilian" emphasis in the booster program, the military had not ceased development of its boosters. In fact, prior to Sputnik I, the military continued to attempt to launch military boosters that would have been necessary to launch such a satellite into orbit. These efforts failed. [52] The Air Force, like the other services, had continued in its efforts to develop multistage rockets. Not until November 1956, when Secretary of the Air Force Quarles issued his order and indicated that no US military satellite would precede a civilian scientific satellite into orbit, did the Air Force cease all vehicle construction and intentionally put its space efforts on hold. [53]

Determining whether Quarles and the Eisenhower administration purposely delayed orbiting a satellite is problematic. Some complained that Eisenhower delayed because he wanted to wait for the development of nonmilitary boosters instead of using existing military boosters. Had the Eisenhower administration clearly indicated to the military services that it desired to be first in space with a satellite, the military might have designed a booster strictly for that purpose. But for the space-for-peace policy, the Eisenhower administration might well have implemented a "crash" program to develop a nonmilitary booster. To conclude that President Eisenhower's space-for-peace proposal, by itself, allowed the USSR to be "first" is speculative at best. Nevertheless, it appears that Quarles was perhaps willing to accept the USSR being first in space so long as the freedom of passage in space principle was established as a result. [54]

The Eisenhower administration's initial response to the two Sputniks was to advance with same due deliberation as it had been proceeding and to treat the Soviet achievement as being "no big deal," in the current vernacular. Eisenhower did perceive a need to demonstrate some success in the missile programs and appointed a panel to study the US missile program. The "fevered tone" and substance of the resulting report of the Security Resources Panel [55] (known as the Gaither Report) helped generate public pressure that caused President Eisenhower to agree to increased spending on missile programs. While a long-term salient impact of the report was increased emphasis on better scientific education and basic research, the Gaither Report also helped give rise to the misperception of a "missile gap" between the United States and the USSR. The USSR may have been ahead in developing satellites and some aspects of missile development, that is, thrust. However, as discussed above, the US was ahead in many important aspects regarding the delivery of weapons of mass destruction by missiles. [56]

Notes

---

[1] Sir Arnold Duncan McNair, Michael R. E. Kerr, and Robert A. MacCrindle, The Law of the Air, 2d ed. (London: Stevens, 1953), appendix, 295-328, cited in Lee Bowen, "An Air Force History of Space Activities 1945-1959" (Washington, D.C.: USAF Historical Division Liaison Office, August 1964), 59; and Col Martin B. Schofield, USAF, "Control of Outer Space," Air University Quarterly Review 10, no. 1 (Spring 1958): 93-104.

[2] John Cobb Cooper, "High Altitude Flight and National Sovereignty," International Law Quarterly Review 4 (July 1951): 411-18.

[3] Bowen, 58-59.

[4] Ibid.

[5] Welf Heinrich, Prince of Hanover, Gesellschaft für Weltraumforschung, "The Legal Problems of Space," trans. Robert W. Schmidt (Maxwell AFB, Ala.: Documentary Research Division, Research Studies Institute, 1953), 1.

[6] The society, founded by the well-known German-Romanian scientist/ mathematician Hermann Oberth, among others, in 1927, eventually became the most influential of the European rocket societies. See David N. Spires, Beyond Horizons: A Half Century of Air Force Space Leadership, rev. ed. (Maxwell AFB, Ala.: Air University Press, 1998), 5.

[*] Heinrich completed his doctor of law thesis entitled "Air Law and Space" in 1953 while at Georg-August University in Göttingen, Germany. His doctoral thesis was a continuation of the work initiated in the 1930s by Vladimir Mandl.

[7] Heinrich, 2-7.

[8] Bowen, 61. Bowen cites "Space Law," a symposium prepared at the request of Senator Lyndon B. Johnson, chairman, Senate Special Committee on Space and Astronautics, 85th Congo 2d sess. 31 December 1958, 129 (hereafter "Space Law"), which in turn cites Oscar Schachter, "Who Owns the Universe?" in Corneilus Ryan, ed., Across the Space Frontiers (New York: Viking Press, 1952).

[9] Project RAND began operating in May 1946 and was initially an independent consulting contractor of the Army Air Forces with Douglas Aircraft Company in Santa Monica, California. RAND was created in 1946 at the direction of Gen Henry H. "Hap" Arnold, commanding general of the US Army Air Forces (AAF). In 1948 Project RAND was reorganized as a nonprofit consulting firm, the RAND Corporation. In 1949 and again in 1951, RAND published studies titled, "Utility of a Satellite Vehicle for Reconnaissance." Over the years, RAND has produced a series of studies for the Air Force and the National Aeronautics and Space Administration (NASA). Between 1946 and 1956, little was accomplished in the actual development of a satellite as contemplated by RAND due in part to fiscal restraints, skepticism within the scientific

12

community, and interservice rivalries. Such rivalry was typified by LeMay's 1946 request to RAND and other actions. (Spires, 14-24.) These rivalries continued into the 1950s with guided missiles spawning contentions. Robert J. Watson, Into the Missile Age, 1956-1960, vol. 4, History of the Office of the Secretary of Defense (Washington, D.C.: Historical Office, Office of the Secretary of Defense, 1997), 40-41. Concurrent development of a booster to launch such a satellite into orbit had not progressed very far and for many of the same reasons.

[10] Gregory W. Pedlow and Donald E. Welzenbach. The CIA and the U-2 Program, 1954-1974 (Langley, Va.: Center for Study of Intelligence, Central Intelligence Agency, 1998), 17.

[11] Air Force Lt Col Richard S. Leghorn, who would later be instrumental in creating Eisenhower's open skies policy, was the Air Force liaison to the study group. In 1946 and 1948 he had presented papers arguing that the United States should develop a high-altitude strategic and tactical reconnaissance capability. Leghorn, an MIT graduate, had served as an Army Air Forces reconnaissance officer in Europe during World War II. After the war, he worked for Eastman Kodak but was recalled to active duty during the Korean War. Initially, in April 1951, he became the head of the Reconnaissance Systems Branch of the Wright Development Command, Dayton, Ohio, but in early 1952 was assigned to the Pentagon staff of Col Bernard A Shriever, assistant for development planning to the Air Force deputy chief of staff for development. In the latter position, Leghorn helped lay the groundwork for what would eventually become the U-2. Members of the study group included Chairman Carl F. P. Overhage (Eastman Kodak), Edward M. Purcell (Harvard University), Saville Davis (Christian Science Monitor), Allen F. Donovan (Cornell Aeronautics Laboratory), Peter C. Goldmark (Columbia Broadcasting System Laboratories), Edwin H. Land (founder, Polaroid Corporation). Stewart E. Miller (Bell Laboratories), Richard S. Perkin (Perkin-Elmer Company), and Louis E. Ridenour (Ridenour Associates), Pedlow and Welzenbach, 4, 6-7, 18.

[12] R. Cargill Hall, "Origins of US Space Policy: Eisenhower, Open Skies, and Freedom of Space," Colloquy (December 1993), 19.

[13] Ibid. Eisenhower was not the first United States official to express concern about a nuclear Pearl Harbor. Gen Henry H. "Hap" Arnold, commanding general of the AAF, had expressed the same concern nearly 10 years earlier. See Spires, 30.

[14] While Eisenhower may have feared a nuclear surprise attack, the primary focus of the US ballistic missile program, even under Eisenhower, was never the launching of a space satellite for intelligence purposes, but rather the creation of a system to deliver a hydrogen warhead on target anywhere on earth.

[15] The Surprise Attack Panel's membership was drawn from the US scientific and engineering communities, including many who had served on the Beacon Hill Study Group. During the time the TCP/Surprise Attack Panel was meeting, the Air Force continued to move forward with a program to develop a reconnaissance satellite system. On 27 November 1954, the Air Force's Research and Development Command had made the decision to pursue a satellite system and on 16 March 1955 had completed a formal statement of objectives. Hall, "Origins," 20. Also see "USAF Space Programs, 1945-1962" (Maxwell AFB, Ala.: USAF Historical Division Liaison Office, undated), 9-10.

[16] Hall, "Origins," 19-20.

[17] Pedlow and Welzenbach, 85.

[18] Hall, "Origins," 6.

[19] Welles Hangen, "Russia Charges Balloon Forays by US & Turks; Reports Inroads by Spheres Equipped with Cameras and Radio Equipment; Leaflets Noted Anew: State Department Suggests Moscow May Refer to Air Force Weather Balloons," New York Times, 6 February 1956: "US Studying Protest," New York Times, 7 February 1956; and Anthony Leviero, "Balloon Activity Explained By US-Air Force Says Some of 200 Loosed in Scotland May Have Drifted to Soviet," New York Times, Special Edition, 9 February 1956.

[20] Elie Abel, "Dulles Hints US Will Try to Curb Balloon Flights: Implies Weather Apparatus Will Be Kept From Soviet Skies as Friendly Move--Espionage Use Denied," special to New York Times, 8 February 1956. "Balloon Flights Stopped by US to Satisfy Soviet," special to New York Times, 9 February 1956.

[21] "Russians Display Balloons of US-Call Flights a Brink-of-War Act-Insist Spying, Not Weather Study, Is Aim," special to New York Times, 10 February 1956.

[22] "Transcript of the Record of News Conference Held by Dulles," New York Times, 8 February 1956.

[23] Charles E. Egan, "Soviet is Accused of Balloon Scare-Air Chief Says Moscow Seeks to Create 'Incident,' Espionage Charge Denied," New York Times, 12 February 1956.

[24] Pedlow and Welzenbach, 85. At the same time the Air Force balloon program was receiving criticism, Richard M. Bissell Jr., special assistant to the Director of Central Intelligence Allen W. Dulles and the CIA official designated by Dulles to oversee the U-2 program, had also decided to use "weather research" as the cover story for the U-2 should its existence ever be made public. Killian and Land disagreed with Bissell's proposed cover story. If a U-2 were ever lost over hostile territory, they proposed that the US "not try to deny responsibility but should state that the U-2 overflights were 'to guard against surprise attack.'" Killian and Land's proposal was to be studied (but never was) and Bissell's weather research cover story remained operative and was implemented vis-à-vis Francis Gary Powers's U-2 (discussed later in chapter 5). Ibid., 89, 178-80.

[25] Ibid., 86. In reality, some balloons were launched to chart the jet stream. However, launching weather related balloons at the same time that intelligence-gathering balloons were launched caused the baby to be thrown out with the bath water.

[26] Hall, "Origins," 21. Hall provides a complete analysis regarding the policy factors impacting the creation of intelligence-gathering satellites during the Eisenhower administration.

[27] IGY was "perhaps the most ambitious and at the same time the most successful cooperative enterprise ever undertaken by nations. The IGY was a scientific year when experts from 67 nations agreed to observe the earth over its whole surface, simultaneously, and with precise instruments designed to the same standards so that the changing phenomena enveloping the earth could be caught and described in their full global sense." See Lloyd V. Berkner, "Foreword," in J. Tuzo Wilson, IGY The Year of the New Moons (New York: Alfred A. Knopf, 1961).

Beginning in 1945, the US had already contemplated a military space program and shortly thereafter studied the feasibility of a US launched satellite. As noted above, the early consideration of a satellite program got lost in a thicket not only of interservice rivalries over custody of such a program but also in skepticism from influential civilian scientists. For a detailed description of the period from 1945 until 1955, see Bowen and Schofield references cited in note 1.

[28] Vechernaya Moskva, "Evening Moscow:" 15 April 55, cited in Harry Schwartz, "Russians Already Striving to Set Up Space Satellite," New York Times, 30 July 1955, 1; and "Soviet Gives No Date," New York Times, 30 July 1955.

[29] For amplification of this point, see Stephen E. Ambrose, Eisenhower, vol. 2, The President (New York: Simon and Shuster, 1984).

[*] Quarles served as assistant secretary of defense for research and development from September 1953 to August 1955. He then served as secretary of the Air Force from August 1955 to April 1957 and became deputy secretary of defense in April 1957 and served in that capacity until May 1959.

[30] Spires, 41

[31] Some historians assert that the Navy, which eventually was selected to manage the development of the nonmilitary booster, was aware of this NSC decision when it submitted its proposal for developing these boosters to the NSC for approval while the Army and Air Force were not. "USAF Space Programs," 12.

[32] "USAF Space Programs," 12-13; Hall, "Origins," 22-23; and Bowen, 57-83.

[33] Raymond W. Young, "The Aerial Inspection Plan and Air Sovereignty," George Washington Law Review 24, no. (5 April 1956): 565-89.

[34] Spires (41) correctly concludes that Eisenhower's civilian IGY satellite was a "stalking horse" to establish the precedent of "freedom in space" for eventual military reconnaissance satellites and focused attention on the former as a diversion from the latter.

[35] . Ibid,; Hall, "Origins," 6, 19-22.

[36] Ibid., 21.

[37] "Open skies" was part of President Eisenhower's space-for-peace policy. Open skies contemplated the sharing of information regarding the exploration of outer space, the setting of limits on sovereignty regarding outer space, and the inspection of space program facilities. In "Origins of US Space Policy," Cargill Hall traces the origin of the open skies doctrine to Richard Leghorn. Leghorn, while working for Eisenhower's special assistant Harold Stassen, had written a paper and subsequently a booklet explaining the disarmament proposal made by Eisenhower at the Geneva Conference. In a 5 August 1955 article in U.S. News & World Report, Leghorn explained the Eisenhower administration's rationale for open skies and its implication for arms reduction. See R. Cargill Hall, "The Eisenhower Administration and the Cold War: Framing American Astronautics to Serve National Security," Prologue, Quarterly of the National Archives 27, no. 1 (Spring 1995): 63-64. Hereafter Hall, "Cold War."

[38] Russell Baker, "US To Launch Earth Satellite 200-300 Miles Into Outer Space; World Will Get Scientific Data," New York Times, 30 July 55, 1.

[39] A. Kislov and S. Krylov, "State Sovereignty in Air Space," International Affairs (Moscow) (March 1956) cited in Maj Howard J. Neumann, USAF, "The Legal Status of Outer Space and the Soviet Union," Space Law, 495-503.

[40] Bowen, 64; Hall, "Cold War," ibid.

[41] Bowen, ibid.

[42] While the first stage of the Vanguard was fully developed and a number successfully launched, three stages of the Vanguard were necessary to launch a satellite into orbit. The second and third stages of the Vanguard never got beyond dummy status.

[43] Marven L. Whipple, "Atlantic Missile Range/Eastern Test Range Index of Missile

Launchings, 1950-1974."

[44] "USAF Space Programs," 15-16.

[45] Bowen, 57-107; Watson, 157-79.

* Sputnik as used hereafter refers specifically to the spaceflights of Sputniks I and II not to the general term sputnik, which is the Russian word for satellite.

[46] Watson, 123-26.

[47] Piers Brendon, Ike, His Life and Times (New York: Harper & Row, 1986), 347-49; Marquis William Childs, Eisenhower: Captive Hero; A Critical Study of the General and the President (New York: Harcourt, Brace, 1958), 258-63.

[48] For a more detailed discussion of the Soviet and US capabilities, see Robert H. Ferrell, American Diplomacy: A History (New York: Norton, 1969), 659-60.

[49] In his first meeting with DOD officials after Sputnik was in orbit, Eisenhower learned from the Army that its Redstone rocket may have been able to launch a US satellite into orbit two months earlier than Sputnik. Further, Eisenhower learned that the Army never made such an attempt because the president had given the mission to the Navy Vanguard program. On 8 October 1957, Eisenhower asked Deputy Secretary of Defense Quarles if the assertion of the Army officials was true. Quarles responded to the effect that the situation was even worse given that the Army could have accomplished the launch two years earlier, had not DOD officials and Quarles himself had decided that it was "better to have the earth satellite proceed separately from military development" so as to "stress the peaceful character of the satellite program." See Ambrose, 428.

[50] Hall, "Origins," 22.

[51] Spires, 47.

[52] Given that the Explorer satellite program successfully launched after Sputnik and given that on 20 September 1956 a Jupiter-C with a Redstone rocket as a first stage plus upper stages like those proposed for the Orbiter had successfully carried an 84-pound payload that could have been replaced by a satellite, Quarles and the Army officials may have been correct when they informed Eisenhower that the United States could have placed an object into orbit before Sputnik. See also Whipple.

[53] Hall, "Origins," 22; Whipple.

[54] Hall, "Origins," 21-22. A valid question, not answered herein, is whether the Eisenhower administration purposefully allowed the USSR to be "first-in-space" to lure the USSR into creating by its own actions the principle of freedom of passage in outer space. Such could explain why Eisenhower assigned to nonexistent nonmilitary boosters, the task of sending a satellite into orbit. Perhaps, Eisenhower knowingly and intentionally proposed an "impossibility." If anyone appears to have had such a design in mind, it appears to have been Air Force secretary (later Deputy Secretary of Defense) Quarles. (See note 36, chapter 2.)

[55] The panel was chaired by H. Rowan Gaither, chairman of the board of directors of the Ford Foundation. For a more complete description of the panel and its membership and its interworkings, see Watson, 136-41.

[56] Ibid., 132-55, 179-87, 293-322.

Chapter 2

Air Force Opposition to International Conventions on Space

The Air Force had a major impact on the evolution of outer space law during the 1950s through its close relationship to the Air Coordinating Committee (ACC). [1] Before Sputnik I, the United States had resisted the efforts of Professor Cooper and others to establish an international convention for outer space. US opposition was, in large part, due to the strong and particularly active role that the Air Force played within the ACC.

Early Air Force Actions Affecting Outer Space Law

The idea for creating the ACC emerged on 26 December 1944. In a memorandum, Assistant Secretary of War for Air Robert A. Lovett [2] recommended establishing an interdepartmental committee "to obtain the information and guidance necessary to make demobilization policies and procedures as effective as possible in preserving the productive capacity required for future national defense." [3] On 27 March 1945, Acting Secretary of State Joseph C. Grew, Secretary of War Henry L. Stimson, Secretary of Navy James Forrestal, and Secretary of Commerce Henry A. Wallace signed the "Interdepartmental Memorandum Regarding Organizing of Air Coordinating Committee." [4] On 19 September 1946, President Harry S Truman issued Executive Order 9781, Establishment of the Air Coordination Committee.

Under Truman's executive order, the Air Coordinating Committee held the authority to establish US policy regarding international law affecting air and outer space. The ACC had authority to take its views directly to the International Civil Aviation Organization (ICAO) as representing those of the United States. [5] Given that the ICAO had a Legal Committee, the ACC created a parallel Legal Subcommittee (later division). The purpose of the subcommittee was to "provide machinery to develop and coordinate the policies which would guide the positions to be taken by the US delegation to the Legal Committee" of the ICAO. [6] The Air Force, which only recently had been separated from the Army, was assigned as the working group for this effort. With the Air Force concurring, the ACC encouraged US compliance with all ICAO recommendations except when, among other reasons, the implementation would be detrimental to the national interest. [7] Until November 1949, the Air Force and Navy had individual service representation on the Legal Subcommittee. At that time single military representation became desirable and an assistant general counsel became the Department of Defense (DOD) member on the subcommittee. [8] While formal membership of the military services on the subcommittee ended, they did not cease active participation in the Legal Subcommittee.

Robert A. Lovett, Assistant
Secretary of War for Air

The importance attached to being an active participant of the ACC is demonstrated by the effort the military services exerted to maintain an active presence at the ACC. In addition to its departmental or secretarial level (Department of the Air Force) representation on the ACC, the Air Force had a staff liaison officer to the ACC. The Air Force also retained membership on the ACC Subcommittees on General ICAO Matters and on the Chicago Convention. In 1952 the Air Force had regained service membership on the Legal Division. However, within the Air Force there was divisiveness regarding its representation at the ACC. Members of the Air Staff had become restive over not receiving adequate coordination from the ACC on issues of importance to the Air Staff. Officials recounted that the Air Force liaison officer had given up membership on the Legal Division to the general counsel of the Air Force. One Air Staff official recommended that an Air Force staff judge advocate be designated as an alternate member to the Legal Division, noting that "Air Force membership on the Legal Division should emanate from the Air Staff." [9] After some discussion, the Air Staff concluded that members of the judge advocate general (JAG) corps should not have to wait for the initiation of coordination. Instead they should take an active approach and "force" consideration of their concerns on the Air Force general counsel representative to the Legal Division.

During the years following the 1944 Chicago Convention, Professor Cooper continued to work and publish on issues associated with sovereignty of airspace and outer space. His works often became the focal points of discussion particularly within the ACC Legal Division. Cooper sought to establish a direct relationship with the Air Coordinating Committee. He wrote Delbert W. Rentzel, chairman, Civil Aeronautics Board, and an ACC member, to inquire whether any ACC attorneys might desire to work under Cooper at the Institute of Air and Space Law-opened in September 1952-at McGill University. [10] By 1955 Professor Cooper had concluded that an international convention similar to the Chicago Convention for airspace was needed for outer space. He supported the principle of freedom of passage in and opposed the assertion of national sovereignty over outer space. Undoubtedly, he would have included such in any convention he proposed; however, there is no assurance that the ICAO would have agreed with Cooper or with his definition as to where outer space began.

Although Cooper and President Dwight D. Eisenhower agreed as to the goal to be achieved, it is unclear to what extent Eisenhower and others in the United States agreed with the point of delimitation that Cooper proposed. The primary divergence between Cooper's proposal and the position of Eisenhower was over how the principle would be established. Whereas Cooper proposed that it be by convention; Eisenhower and the Air Force preferred that the law be derived by custom and practice. Eisenhower's goal had apparently not been shared with or been digested by many military officials in the Air Force. Thus, certain Air Force officers periodically made statements contrary to the freedom of passage principle.

During the spring of 1956, Cooper met with ACC chairman Louis S. Rothschild.[*] Because of that meeting, Ronald C. Kinsey, secretary of the ACC Legal Division, requested answers to the following questions:

> Should the ACC consider and recommend US positions re-outer atmospheric space in relation to sovereignty problems raised by use of present and future rockets and missiles?
>
> Could a legal panel be useful?
>
> When a US position is determined should there be an international convention? [11]

Kinsey noted that in addition to Cooper, Oscar Schachter, C. Wilfred Jenks, and Andrew J. Haley (director and general counsel of the American Rocket Society)[†] had proposed the above questions given that Cooper and others had placed the general subject of outer space sovereignty on the agenda for the Tenth Session of the World Assembly of the ICAO to be held in Caracas, Venezuela, in June 1956. [12] On 7 March 1956 the Legal Division met and considered these questions, With the Air Force representative strongly concurring, the division concluded that "the problems posed by Mr. Cooper's questions involve extremely important policy as well as legal considerations, Security aspects, and the possible need for a non-traditional type of approach, would make it imperative that the matter be kept flexible pending further study by the United States." [13]

The ACC Legal Division further concluded that consideration of the issues by an international body was premature and that the United States should consider the important policy problems within its own government prior to endorsing such international action. Finally, the division recommended that the US object to even the study of the matter by an international body as being premature. These recommendations did not sway Cooper and he pressed his position to the point that, in an April press release, the ICAO announced the need for an international agreement on outer space sovereignty. [14] Air Force officials perceived that Cooper was "agitating" for an international convention on outer space. [15] As a result, US government officials became concerned that not

---

[*] Rothschild served concurrently as under secretary of commerce.

[†] Jenks was an associate of Cooper's at the Institute of International Law, whose thesis proposed sovereignty as high as three hundred miles above the earth's surface. In contrast, Haley appeared to argue that sovereignty extended into areas traversed by any proposed satellite.

just discussion of the general issue but that a convention might be placed on the agenda at the upcoming ICAO world assembly. [16]

The Air Force representative at the ACC, Assistant Secretary for Materiel Dudley C. Sharp,[*] responded to Cooper's proposal by writing ACC Chairman Rothschild. Noting that the proposal entered an "uncharted area of thinking [and] cut across certain high-level policies…such as the President's mutual inspection proposal, the recent Air Force weather balloon problem, earth satellite projects, and guided missile testing projects," Sharp recommended that the ACC postpone consideration of the proposal. He argued that until higher-level policies had been developed, the Air Coordinating Committee consider only "appropriate means whereby such higher-level policy considerations can be isolated and promptly considered." Finally, Sharp proposed that the United States adopt a position at the ICAO seeking to have the matter postponed as being premature. Sharp argued that Cooper's proposition posed a "number of problems which should properly be disposed of at the National Security Council or Presidential level" before being considered by the ACC. Once such national security issues were resolved, Sharp indicated he felt comfortable with the ACC dealing with the issue and allowing legal experts to "attack the problem of drafting a United States position on any proposed international convention." [17] At the same time, Secretary Sharp asked Air Force chief of staff Gen Nathan F. Twining for Air Staff "views on the military implications of an international convention regarding the use of outer air space." Sharp encouraged the other services to also review the issue. [18]

---

[*] Sharp later became secretary of the Air Force, serving from 11 December 1959 to 20 January 1961.

Dudley C. Sharp. Sharp served in various high-level offices in the Air Force, eventually becoming secretary of the Air Force in 1959.

In letters dated 9 and 10 April 1956 to Chairman Rothschild, Cooper encouraged the ACC to reject the position of its own Legal Division. [19] Given Eisenhower's July 1955 statement that the United States would include a satellite as part of its IGY effort, Cooper argued that the US had precipitated the need to resolve the issue of sovereignty by announcing its intention to launch a satellite into outer space. Cooper felt that if the US was prepared to launch such a satellite, it ought also to be prepared to state its position on the sovereignty issue. In a second letter, Cooper reiterated his earlier position. He reasoned that the United States, by announcing its intention to launch a satellite, had accepted the proposition that it did not retain sovereignty of the outer space above its territory and thereby waived any legitimate grounds on which to object to foreign satellites passing over its territory. Cooper's argument was clearly in accord with President Eisenhower's position of espousing a freedom of passage in outer space, but the president's position and its implications had apparently not yet been communicated outside a small circle of advisors. Given Professor Cooper's efforts, ACC Chairman Rothschild quickly responded to Secretary Sharp's request. Rothschild reiterated the positions taken by Kinsey and the Legal Division and welcomed Air Force and other DOD input when the studies Sharp had initiated were completed. [20]

Cooper was not about to let the issue die based on the ACC's actions. In an address to the annual convention of the American Society of International Law (ASIL), he discussed the issues associated with outer space sovereignty and urged that outer space law issues be resolved through an international convention. Also at the ASIL convention, Professor Cooper proposed, among other things, a convention providing that all space above "contiguous space," that is, three hundred miles above the earth's surface, be free for the passage of all devices. Perhaps because of its premature nature, but for reasons unknown, Cooper's proposal did not pass.

In the meantime, by memorandum dated 9 May 1956, Col Paul W. Norton, director of civil law, Office of the Judge Advocate General, responded to the request by Sharp and General Twining for an Air Force position. Colonel Norton informed Maj Gen Richard C. Lindsay, acting assistant deputy chief of staff for operations, that any international convention was "premature and contrary to the best interests of the Air Force." Noting that the United States had "assumed the lead in the research and development of long-range guided missiles, rockets, and satellite programs," Norton advised that "any codification of formal, intergovernmental rules at this time would operate to fetter the unbounded use of outer space for military research and development." He based this conclusion on the fact that current US programs were military sponsored and that past international conventions regarding airspace allowed military overflights only with special authorization of the subjacent nation. Norton concluded that a like provision would be included in any convention dealing with outer space.

Colonel Norton argued that, given that the United States was more advanced than any other nation, the effect of such a convention would have a more profound effect on the US than on anyone else, including the USSR. He cited case law stating that any nation can take any reasonable and necessary measures to protect its national security even outside its territory and airspace. Based on these legal precedents, he concluded that should foreign use of outer space jeopardize its security then the United States, for its self-defense, could undertake reasonable and necessary unilateral restrictions on the use of space by other nations. Norton argued that other nations would accept such moves and that the US should be prepared to accept similar restrictions if imposed by other nations. He contended that so long as other nations did not raise objection to US programs and no other nation's program presented a threat to the United

States, any international convention would hamper Air Force missions and research. Finally, he advised:

> In this formative stage, we believe the practice of nations will create a more realistic precedent for future conduct in outer space than formulation at this time of international rules which could not possibly be grounded in actual practices and experience, but only on the abstract theories of each country's statesmen and jurists. The value of actual practice is especially important so long as the United States has the capability of leading the way in establishing the precedent. [21]

Maj Hamilton DeSaussure and Maj Gen Albert M. Kuhfeld. DeSaussure prepared key position papers for the Air Force JAG office in support of the Air Force's position in the early debates about outer space. General Kuhfeld later became The Judge Advocate General of the Air Force and was a leading advocate of the Air Force taking a proactive posture in attempting to shape international law as it related to outer space.

Colonel Norton's early pronouncement of an Air Force position opposing Cooper's efforts had been analyzed and written by Maj

Hamilton DeSaussure. [22] Ironically, Major DeSaussure had been Cooper's student, having been a member of the first class to graduate from McGill University's Institute of Air and Space Law.

At the June 1956 ICAO meeting, as a result of the recommendations of the Air Force and others, the US "took the position that international discussion was at that time premature." Generally, the US sentiments were shared by other nations and Cooper's proposal was tabled. [23] However,

> the [Legal] Commission [of the ICAO] noted the growing interest among jurists in the problems concerning "Outer space." [The Commission] considers that these problems fall essentially within the province of the functions of the Organization and that, at a suitable time, they might be included in the general work program of the Legal Committee. [24]

In its 1956 Annual Report to the President, the ACC related that its Legal Division had formulated the US position for discussions regarding the legal problems of outer space in preparation for the ICAO meeting in Caracas. The ACC reported: "Among other things in its position, the United States delegation strongly opposed inclusion of the topic 'Legal Problems beyond Air Space' in the work program of the ICAO Legal Committee on the ground that there is insufficient knowledge at the present time of the practical problems for which a solution may be necessary." [25]

Air Force Actions before and after Sputnik

In January 1957, during his State of the Union message, President Eisenhower expressed a willingness to accept an international agreement to control missile and satellite development for use in outer space. He linked this position to his space-for-peace and disarmament proposals. [26] Later that month, during a disarmament debate, Henry Cabot Lodge, US ambassador to the United Nations (UN), reconfirmed such US willingness. Lodge noted that several nations were proceeding to launch objects into outer space and that some form of international control needed to be established. [27]

Shortly after Eisenhower's State of the Union address, in an air intelligence report entitled "The Legal Status of Outer Space and the

Soviet Union" (approved by Col Clifford R. Opper, Air Force director of intelligence), Maj Howard J. Neumann discussed international law and the Soviet interpretation of outer space. [28] Major Neumann noted that while the Soviets claimed unlimited sovereignty to all space (air and outer) over its territory, the Chicago Convention* was premised on the 1919 Paris Convention's † use of the French words meaning atmospheric space. Accordingly, Major Neumann argued that outer space was governed by no existing law. He pointed out that the USSR, which was not a party to either convention, did not limit its sovereignty to the stratosphere.

Major Neumann concluded that "an international convention seems to be necessary at an early stage of mankind's penetration and exploration of outer space, in order to prevent undesirable interferences which end in loss of human lives and valuable material." [29] Contrary to the Air Force position at the ACC, Major Neumann concluded that Cooper's proposal had merit and advised that, since the USSR had projects planned for outer space, it might be possible to conclude an international agreement with the USSR establishing the legal status of outer space. If the issue were not resolved, Major Neumann predicted that it would serve as a "constant source of international complications." [30]

The sovereignty issue was raised again during the summer of 1957. Col T. J. Dayharsh of the Permanent Joint Board of Defense (Canada and the United States), questioned Howard E. Hensleigh, assistant DOD general counsel for international affairs, regarding the legality of proposed flights of US intercontinental ballistic missiles through the "upper air space" over Canada. Hensleigh in turn requested assistance on Colonel Dayharsh's request from the DOD military departments. In July, responding on behalf of the Air Force, Charles L. Kent, assistant general counsel, provided Hensleigh with substantive comments including references to the 1956 ICAO assembly and the success of the US in stripping outer space issues from the ICAO agenda. Hensleigh incorporated several of Kent's suggestions including the ICAO reference in a memorandum to Dayharsh indicating that there was no internationally accepted line of demarcation between air and outer space. That fall Dayharsh thanked Hensleigh, noting that his "excellent

---

* Convention on International Civil Aviation.
† The 1919 Parts Convention (International Convention for Air Navigation) addressed International regulation of civilian aerial navigation. It established the International Commission for Aerial Navigation, which was superseded in 1947 by the ICAO.

background material and advice on a desirable United States position was made available to briefing officers and used by them in briefing selected Canadians." Colonel Dayharsh noted that the "Canadian viewpoint coincides with that approach to the question recommended [by Hensleigh]" and that all issues had been satisfactorily resolved. [31]

The Soviets launched Sputnik I on 4 October 1957 and Sputnik II in November. During the several months before the launchings, "there was furious activity on the Air Staff on space matters." [32] The Air Staff was preparing for an Air Force space launch of a "civilian" satellite at Cape Canaveral.[*] During this time, the legal ramifications of the launch were being studied, particularly the issue of whether an orbit over another country would violate its sovereignty. The JAG's International Law Division advised the Air Staff to the effect that there was no answer to the sovereignty issue "because no spacecraft had ever been successfully launched and no international agreement existed on the subject." [33] Neither practice nor treaty was yet in effect.

Having learned of the Soviet's successful launch and orbit of Sputnik, several Air Staff members rushed to the office of General LeMay, the vice chief of staff. Having briefed him on the Soviet launch, they questioned him as to whether the US should protest given that by Sputnik's overflight of the United States the Soviets had violated US sovereignty. He responded, "We were going to orbit their country weren't we?" [34] His reply ended any Air Force-initiated protest of the Soviet launch. [†] Deputy Secretary of Defense Donald Quarles observed, "the Russians have done us a good turn, unintentionally, in establishing the concept of freedom of international space…Eisenhower…looked ahead and asked about a reconnaissance vehicle [satellite]." [35] During a news conference on 9 October 1957, Eisenhower hinted at his stalking-horse agenda when questioned regarding Sputnik. He stated, "From what they

---

[*] As noted earlier, by the mid-1940s, there was already significant interservice rivalry seeking to capture the space program. Indicative that this rivalry continued well into the 1950s. Air Force vice chief of staff General LeMay would state on 17 March 1959 that "while recognizing Army and Navy interest in aerospace projects, we would seek to limit their participation to a coordinating role."

[†] General LeMay's position was clearly in accord with Eisenhower's thinking. Whether General LeMay was advised as to the stalking-horse strategy or separately came to the same conclusion is unknown. If he had been advised, General LeMay apparently had not shared that insight with others in the Air Force such as Generals Donald L. Putt and Richard M. Montgomery, both of whom, as discussed below, took much different positions.

say they have put one small ball in the air;" and, he added, "at this moment you [don't] have to fear the intelligence aspects of this." [36]

By tying the US space program to his freedom of space policy, Eisenhower had hoped to impress upon the world the peaceful intent of the US.[*] However, whatever propaganda advantage the United States had gained by such peaceful remonstrations was overshadowed when the USSR was "first in space." Interestingly, the launch of Sputnik, while sharpening the focus of the heretofore essentially academic discussion of sovereignty in outer space, did not result in any immediate international convention. Additionally, the Soviets reversed their position of asserting sovereignty over outer space above their territory. When confronted with their apparent reversal, the Soviets adopted temporarily the rather specious position (clearly contrary to the laws of physics and astronautics) that it had not violated any other nation's sovereignty since Sputnik had not flown over any nation's territory but instead the territories had passed under Sputnik. Eisenhower's hidden stalking-horse agenda of obtaining free passage in space for intelligence gathering devices had been achieved. The US was not alone in failing to object to Sputnik's overflight of its territory. No other country objected to the overflight of their territory either, thus establishing the first custom in outer space law, that is, the free flight of objects in outer space. The USSR, in its exuberance over its successful satellite launches, made no distinction between scientific and intelligence-gathering devices (nor did any other country). When countries failed to object to subsequent satellite overflights, the custom became firmly established. [37]

Because of Sputnik I, ICAO President Walter Binaghi wrote to Nelson B. David, the US representative on the ICAO Council, inquiring whether it was time to finally consider the issue of outer space sovereignty. He also inquired as to the ICAO's appropriateness as the vehicle to do so. Binaghi's inquiry was referred to the ACC by David. Robert Kinsey, secretary of the ACC Legal Division, informed the members of the division of Binaghi's letter and set the matter for consideration at the next meeting. On 8 November 1957, the ACC's Legal Division, with the Air Force concurring, approved a position in response to Binaghi's inquiry. Before forwarding this response, the division reviewed the earlier US

---

[*] Again it must be remembered that the focus of the us missile program was not focused on launching a satellite but rather focused on delivery of a warhead on target anywhere on earth.

opposition to the inclusion of the sovereignty issue in the ICAO's work program.

The Air Force, represented by Daggett Howard, associate general counsel for international civil aviation affairs, and the Army argued that the main US interest in space was military. Howard, who later would become the first general counsel for the Federal Aviation Administration, indicated that it was problematic to have the ICAO undertake discussion of the sovereignty issue when the USSR-the only state to have launched a satellite-was not a member of the body. [38] The division approved a letter to David stating:

> The United States believes that considerably more technical development and experience are needed before any international action on the problem you have raised should be undertaken. Rules and regulations or theories relating to international principles applicable to outer space evolved in this early stage could do little to further the work. They might put unnecessary and undesirable obstacles in its path. [39]

The division noted that, given that the predominant interest in outer space was not civil aviation, the ICAO was not the appropriate vehicle to undertake resolution of the sovereignty issue. The Legal Division stated that "it is too early to predict what methods for dealing with this problem may prove to be desirable." Binaghi later advised David that he had sent the same letter to the United Kingdom (which never responded), France (which desired ICAO discussion), and Canada (which supported the US position but felt the United Nations was the appropriate vehicle). While noting that other countries desired an ICAO discussion of the sovereignty issue, Binaghi indicated an understanding of the US position and agreed to delay any further discussion of the subject until the ICAO's next session. [40]

Subsequently, in a letter to Henry T. Snowden, chief, Aviation Division, Department of State, David agreed that there was little practicality in the ICAO studying the space problems at this time, but pointed out that the United States could not "count on keeping ICAO's head in the sand on this issue. A more realistic attitude would be to prepare for ICAO consideration of the subject and to develop a positive approach as to how we want to have this done." [41] Later the ICAO discussed the subject of outer space and agreed that it had authority to conduct studies of the subject matter. However, the ICAO took no formal action.

Daggett Howard and Secretary of the Air Force James Douglas (1958). Howard represented the Air Force at International Civil Aviation Organization meetings to discuss sovereignty issues in outer space. He became the general counsel of the Federal Aviation Administration.

In January 1958 the ACC Legal Division met with David to consider past and future ICAO discussions regarding outer space. David enumerated the reasons why he expected the ICAO to reverse direction and eventually take up the issue. During the meeting, the Air Force was the most vociferous opponent of any shift in the US position. Howard again forcefully represented the Air Force point of view that efforts to develop outer space law should not be adopted before any actual operations that such laws would be intended to govern had begun. He reiterated that the main issues regarding outer space involved "national defense and military type questions."

Howard asserted that the ICAO was an inappropriate vehicle for discussing the issue since the Soviets were not members of the ICAO. He argued that it would be dangerous for the free world to adopt restrictions on its own space activities without the Eastern bloc's participation. Since

30

the Soviet bloc had yet to agree on issues impacting airspace, Howard maintained that there was no need to do for outer space what had yet to be done for airspace. Nonetheless, he argued that the ICAO could not held at bay indefinitely. He argued that from a negotiating standpoint, it was stronger to take a firm negative position rather than open the door slightly to discussions, which when once begun, likely could not be contained. David indicated agreement with the Air Force position but noted that the arguments given by the Air Force had not persuaded other ICAO council members.

Finally, Howard argued that President Eisenhower's pronouncement that the UN and not the ICAO should consider the issues surrounding the use of outer space could serve to delay ICAO action on the issue. David agreed that if the issue could be more firmly planted at the UN, the ICAO could be easily dissuaded, and he acknowledged that he understood that the ACC Legal Division essentially sided with the Air Force position. The Legal Division then directed that the State Department, with assistance from the Air Force, prepare a new set of instructions. The instructions would be used by embassies in ICAO Council countries to support the US position of avoiding ICAO discussion of outer space law. [42]

Even though the Air Force had succeeded in keeping outer space law questions off the ICAO agenda and in general had effectively stalled any resolution of outer space law issues, by mid-1958 "the magnitude and variety of these [space law] studies moved several well-known American jurists to remark that the law of space, instead of lagging behind the astronauts as some lawyers fear, is threatening to outfly the attraction of the earth's gravity." [43] State Department officials realized that some guidance was needed for its delegation at the UN. [44]

At this time, State Department legal adviser Loftus Becker proposed a presidential proclamation recognizing that reconnaissance satellites were in accord with international law so long as they did not interfere with terrestrial activity. Hancock expressed his concerns about this wording directly to Becker. Hancock indicated no problem with "snoopniks," but he did question whether the breadth of the proclamation might preclude US objections to future satellites interfering with communication transmissions or weather operations. Hancock asked that Becker confine the proposed proclamation to projects that were part of the IGY. Hancock reasoned that, by following his advice, the US could still contribute to establishing the thrust of the proclamation as a principle of international law without being bound by a premature, unqualified proposition whose consequences were unforeseeable. Hancock did not oppose banning satellites designed for "weapons purposes" as long as the language clearly prohibited any satellites that interfered with any terrestrial activity. [45]

Hancock was not alone in the Air Force in expressing reservations about Becker's proposed proclamation. However, it is not clear that the concerns of the Air Doctrine Branch, which were raised with the director of plans, were made known outside the Air Force. [46] In response to Becker's 3 December draft memorandum for the secretary of state, the DOD assistant general counsel for international affairs, Monroe Leigh, wrote to Becker. Leigh stated that "the proposed proclamation is not as guarded as it should be in order to take care of the interests of various Department of Defense programs." Leigh felt that language excluding objects or vehicles "designed or equipped for weapons purposes" should be revised to prohibit vehicles "intended to inflict injury or damage." Since the US satellite programs were in large part funded by the military, Leigh noted that without his revision Becker's language would create "an almost irrebuttable presumption" that the projects were being carried out for "weapons purposes." Leigh opposed using the law of the high seas as an analogy for developing the law of outer space. Becker included Hancock's IGY proposal and removed the "designed for weapons purposes" language from the draft proclamation. [47] Ironically, just before the US issued the proclamation, East Germany protested the orbiting of US military reconnaissance satellites that were not IGY affiliated. The proclamation was never issued.[*]

The Air Force position and now the US position as established by the ACC and its Legal Division-that ICAO consideration of outer space was premature-remained constant throughout 1958. Eventually, the forum for discussion of outer space issues shifted from the ICAO to the UN. As a result, and in large part due to strong Air Force urging, the United States had successfully deflected ICAO discussion of the sovereignty issue. As early as 1959, the UN first considered and identified the question of the definition of outer space as a legal problem. In 1959, in accord with US policy, the United Nations Committee on the Peaceful Uses of Outer Space (COPUOS) concluded that a determination of precise limits for

---

[*] By late 1958, the position advocated by the US Air Force of not encouraging the passage of international conventions was more in accord with the position advocated by the USSR than with the US Department of State presumably because both the Air Force and the USSR were more interested in allowing technology to develop.

airspace and outer space was not a problem requiring priority attention. As recently as 1985, the UN (with the ICAO monitoring the progress) again unsuccessfully attempted to define outer space. The issue still remains on the agenda of the Legal Subcommittee of the UN Committee on Peaceful Uses of Outer Space. To date the UN has not defined outer space nor resolved the concomitant sovereignty issue. Given that the delimitation issue is inextricably tied to the sovereignty issue, as long as the Bogota Declaration continues under discussion, the delimitation issue will remain a hot topic.

Project RAND:
Supporting the Air Force Position

Sputniks I and II caused a change in the "discussion of the character of space law and affected the quantity but not the quality of legal writing"; the emphasis of space law discussions "shifted toward a more realistic approach." [48] Apparently Leon Lipson, when making this statement, was not aware of the ongoing discussions being held at the ACC and within the National Security Council (NSC). Contrary to Lipson's October 1959 assertion, US policy making at the ACC and NSC with respect to outer space law was indeed realistic during the 1950s.

Due in part to Sputnik and the growing pressure on the ICAO to address the issue of outer space law, the Air Force recognized that it needed an in-depth analysis of these issues. The Air Force understood the need for this study even though it had been instrumental in successfully delaying the ICAO's consideration of a convention on outer space law. In 1957, at the request of the Air Staff, Project RAND published preliminary findings and recommendations in an interim report entitled "Some Implications for US National Security of Activities in Outer Space." The premise of the RAND study was that the US "would soon have to take a position publicly on questions of sovereignty and associated legal rights and privileges in regard to the use of outer space by nations." The conclusion and recommendations of Project RAND were

Considerations of international law as such ought not now to occupy a major place in the determination of US policies affecting activities by nations in outer space. Existing legal rules do not necessarily require or forbid any specific activities of the type that we are likely to contemplate in outer space; the law of outer space has still to be evolved; the United States should determine what space policies and activities are desirable on other grounds before asking whether they violate old legal rules or require new ones.

Political and psychological measures should be prepared for the contingency of continued Soviet successes in space.

Efforts should be made to offset Russia's claims that it stands only for peace while the US wants war.

The disclosure of news about space activities by the US can be planned to restore confidence abroad in US statements and to further US policy objectives.

To achieve the most favorable political and psychological effects from US activities in space and effectively to frustrate Soviet objectives requires planning and coordination at the highest levels of government. [49]

The RAND report further noted that the initial questions posed concerned "space law," "sovereignty," and associated questions of international law. RAND's conclusions were similar to what the Air Force had been articulating at the ACC, namely, that "the legal approach to developing national policies on space matters is not the only, or even the principal, relevant approach." RAND observed that the most important conclusion was that "considerations of international law as such ought not now to occupy a major place in the determination of US policies affecting activities by nations in outer space." The study suggested that the United States determine what space activities or policies were desired on other grounds before asking if the activities or policies violated old legal rules or required new ones. [50] Finally, the Project RAND report asserted that at the time Sputnik was launched, activities in outer space were not covered by existing international law. [51]

Subsequent to the RAND report, Assistant Secretary of Defense for International Security Affairs Mansfield D. Sprague[*] circulated an outline entitled "Some Elements Requiring Consideration in Formulating a National Policy on Outer Space." Its basic thrust was consistent with the RAND study, stating that "there is a real danger that we may harm ourselves by too early commitments, before the full implications of space

---

[*] Sprague had been an active member of the panel that was responsible for the Gaither Report.

potentials are known. Our policy and national interest should be permitted to develop first: the law, and commitments should follow, and be consonant with the former." [52] However, the outline did note that with respect to the principle of freedom of space that "we must evolve a workable theory of international law" on this problem. [53]

Whether space law should be codified remained an issue. In May 1958, during testimony before the Senate Special Committee on Space and Astronautics, Department of State legal adviser Loftus Becker, echoing what the Air Force had first advised, reiterated US policy.

> It has been felt that the soundest way to progress in the extremely complex field of the law is by means of specific decisions on specific questions presented by specific fact situation…Moreover, there are very great risks in attempting to transmute a body of law based upon one determined set of facts into a body of law with respect to which the basic facts have not been determined. [54]

Accordingly, Becker indicated the State Department was "inclined to view with great reserve" codification of outer space law. [55]

In March 1958, Air Force chief of staff Gen Thomas D. White publicly opposed the setting of any boundaries between air and outer space. General White articulated an air-space continuum (aerospace) doctrine that "it should be recognized that there is no division, per se, between the two. For all practical purposes air and space merge, forming a continuous and indivisible field of operations." [56] Also in the spring of 1958, the assistant deputy chief of staff for plans and programs directed that the Air Doctrine Branch complete a second sovereignty study for Air Force "eyes only," regarding the feasibility of international law for space and its effects on military space programs. The Air Doctrine Branch, Air Policy Division, Directorate of Plans, DCS for Plans and Programs, circulated the study to the Air Staff on 22 August 1958. The study-prepared with the advice and assistance of all interested headquarters agencies, the Air University (AU), and RAND-was circulated among Headquarters USAF offices in October. [57] Given that an earlier published AU study was "divergent" from the opinions of the Air Staff, the Air Doctrine Branch recommended any further studies incorporating the opinions of both be held in abeyance pending completion of the RAND study, which had earlier been circulated in preliminary form.[*] The Air Doctrine Branch study group members recommended that their conclusions form the basis for Air Force policy on the question of sovereignty over outer space.[58]

In February 1959 General White reiterated the continuum doctrine in testimony before the House Committee on Science and Astronautics when he stated, "Since there is no dividing line, no natural barrier separating these two areas (air and space), there can be no operational boundary between them. Thus air and space comprise a single continuous operational field in which the Air Force must continue to function. The area is aerospace."[59] Because he used the term aerospace, General White received some sharp criticism from members of the other services, in the press, and from Congress. He never retracted the term and the criticism eventually subsided. Clearly, the Air Force had dug in its heels on defining where outer space began. While recognizing that international conventions regarding outer space law might be forth-coming the Air Force was not, about to encourage their adoption.

Gen Thomas .C. White. As chief of staff of the Air Force he coined the term aerospace doctrine.

The struggle between those desiring to see the development of outer space law based on custom and precedent and those seeking resolution

[*] For a detailed extract of the Air Doctrine Branch study conclusions, see appendix B.

through limited international agreements continued well into the 1960s. The proponents of the latter, generally jurists and high-level government officials, perceived that eventually "a formal legal code embracing large segments of space activity" could and should be adopted immediately. The proponents of the former approach continued to argue that more scientific facts were needed before decisions could be made and national security might be compromised as a result of such ignorance. These proponents were generally midlevel US government officials. [60]

---

[1] According to the Military Air Transport Service (MATS) history for January-June 1955, the Air Coordinating Committee (ACC) and the Air Force had a close working relationship. The ACC was eventually composed of representatives of the Departments of State, Air Force, Post Office, Navy, and Commerce as well as the Civil Aeronautics Board. It was tasked with assuring that the United States achieve "lasting preeminence in the skies." Specifically, the ACC was used to enable various "segments of the federal executive branch to develop and present an integrated policy on the economic, technical, legal, and diplomatic problems relative to the production and operation of civil and military aircraft in foreign and domestic flight." Walter H. Wager described the ACC as "holding the key to the United States air policy" and as being an effective instrument for the formulation of policy because "it works." Wager, "The Air Coordinating Committee," Air University Quarterly Review 2, no. 4 (Spring 1949).

[2] Lovett, who would eventually become secretary of defense, had served since 1942 on the War Aviation Committee, the forerunner for the ACC, along with the assistant secretaries for air of the Navy and Commerce Departments and the chairman of the Civil Aeronautics Board. See Wager, 18-19.

[3] Kenneth C. Royall, under secretary of war, to assistant secretary of war for air, Memorandum, subject: Air Coordinating Committee, 19 June 1946; and Wager, 21.

[4] Wager, 20.

[5] MATS History, vol. 1, January-June 1955, 4.

[6] ACC Document 51/29.13, 3 February 1948.

[7] Lt Col A. S. Raudabaugh to Col W. Bryte, memorandum, subject: US Matters-General Policy for US Compliance with and Implementation of the Convention and ICAO Decisions Thereunder, Reaffirmation of ACC 52/13, SPM 13 Amended, 4 February 1948.

[8] Lt Col Thomas C. Hollick, assistant executive, DCS/Plans and Operations, to Orders Section, Air Adjutant General, memorandum, subject: Reorganization of the Air Coordinating Committee, 1 December 1949.

[9] Helen Cross (AFOPD-PY-CA) to Colonels Bridges and Cage, memorandum, subject: Air Staff Representation on the Legal Division, ACC, 7 May 1952.

[10] John C. Cooper to Delbert W. Rentzel, chairman, Civil Aeronautics Board, 16 April 1952.

[11] Ronald C. Kinsey, secretary, Legal Division, memorandum, subject: Treatment of the Problem of Sovereignty and Associated Legal Privileges and Rights in Regard to the Use Of Outer Space by Nations, 7 March 1956 (hereafter Kinsey memo).

[12] Ibid.

[13] ACC Legal Division, to ACC executive secretary, draft memorandum, subject: Legal-Treatment of the Problem of Sovereignty and Associated Legal Privileges and Rights in Regard to the Use of "Outer Space" by Nations, 12 March 1956, 1. This memorandum summarizes Legal Division agreements reached at its 7 March 1956 meeting. Kinsey memo cited at note 11 is attached to the ACC memorandum dated 12 March 1956.

[14] News Release, L. C. Boussard, public information officer, International Civil Aviation Organization, Montreal, Canada, 4 April 1956.

[15] Maj Hamilton DeSaussure, memorandum for file, AFCJA, 7 May 1956.

[16] Joseph M. Goldsen and Leon S. Lipson, "Some Implications for US National Security of Activities in Outer Space-An Interim Report," RM 2004 (Santa Monica, Calif.: RAND, 28 October 1957), 1.

[17] Dudley C. Sharp, assistant secretary of the Air Force, to Louis S. Rothschild, ACC chairman, memorandum, subject: Growing Interest in Possible International Convention on Use of "Outer Space" by Nations, 4 April 1956.

[18] Ibid., 2.

[19] John C. Cooper to Louis S. Rothschild, 9 April and 10 April 1956.

[20] Rothschild, chairman, Air Coordinating Committee, to Sharp, Air Force member, ACC, 12 April 1956.

[21] Col Paul W. Norton to Maj Gen Richard C. Lindsay, memorandum, subject: Growing Interest in Possible International Convention on Use of "Outer Space" by Nations, 9 May 1956.

[22] Author's notes no oral interviews with Will H. Carroll and Maj Hamilton DeSaussure.

[23] Goldsen and Lipson, 2.

[24] Report and Minutes of the Legal Commission Document, 1956 International Civil Aviation Organization 7712, A10-LE/5, 6.

[25] Annual Report to the President, Air Coordinating Committee, 1956.

[26] "Text of President Eisenhower's Annual Message to Congress on the State of the Union," New York Times, 11 January 1957.

[27] Maj Howard J. Neumann, "Outer Space and the Soviet Union," Air Intelligence Report, 18 February 1957, 2.

[28] Ibid., 7.

[29] Ibid., 10.

[30] Ibid., 11.

[31] Col T. J. Dayharsh to Howard E. Hensleigh, DOD assistant general counsel (international affairs), memorandum, subject: Canadian Understanding of United States Inter-Continental Ballistic Missile Plans as They Concern Canada, 12 September 1957.

[32] Carroll, 2.

[33] Ibid., 2-3.

[34] Ibid., 3.

[35] R Cargill Hall, "Origins of US Space Policy: Eisenhower, Open Skies, and Freedom of Space," Colloquy (December 1993), 23. Walter A. McDougall, The Heavens and the Earth: A Political History of the Space Age (New York: Basic Books. 1985), 134.

[36] Public Papers of the President of the United States: Dwight David Eisenhower, 1957 (Washington. D.C.: Government Printing Office, 1958 [210]), 724. Whether the Eisenhower administration had simply been willing to accept the Soviets being "first in space" or purposely calculated by playing Br'er Rabbit to the Soviets Br'er Bear, thereby, suckering the Soviets into going first in space so as to set the precedent

Eisenhower wanted to achieve, that is, the freedom of passage in outer space, is unknown but doubtful. However, if anyone had created the scenario for the Soviets to go first in space, it appears to have been DOD civilian officials and Quarles in particular. Quarles recommended the stalking-horse strategy. Quarles issued the gag order on the discussion of military space operations. Quarles directed that no military satellite would precede a US civilian satellite both before and even after Sputnik. Finally, Quarles explained to Eisenhower, shortly after Sputnik's success, how the Soviets had "done us a good turn, unintentionally, by establishing the concept of freedom of international space." See Stephen E. Ambrose, Eisenhower, vol. 2, The President (New York: Simon and Shuster, 1984, 248). If Eisenhower had consciously been setting the Soviets up to go first in space, it is unlikely that Quarles would have felt compelled to explain to Eisenhower the advantage to the US from having the Soviets go first.

[37] Maj John Morrison-Orton, USAF, "Juridical Control of Weapons in Outer Space," (master's thesis, National Law Center, George Washington University, 30 September 1984), 32.

[38] Minutes, 74th Meeting, Legal Division, ACC, 8 November 1957, Agenda Item 1 - ICAO Matters-Treatment of the Problem of Sovereignty and Associated Legal Privileges and Rights in Regard to Use of "Outer Space" by Nations (LD Memo 18-57), 2-4.

[39] William E. Neumeyer, ACC executive secretary, to Nelson David, US representative to ICAO, teletype, 13 November 1957. Attached to Kinsey to ACC Legal Division members, memorandum (LD 18A-57), subject: ICAO Matters-Treatment of the Problem of Sovereignty and Associated Legal Privileges and Rights in Regard to the Use of "Outer Space" by Nations, 14 November 1957.

[40] Nelson David, US representative to ICAO, memorandum of telephone conversation with Alberta Colclaser, State Department representative to ACC Legal Division, and Joan Gravatte, 22 November 1957. Attached to Kinsey to Legal Division members, memorandum (LD 186-57), subject: ICAO Matters-Treatment of the Problem of Sovereignty and Associated Legal Privileges and Rights in Regard to the Use of "Outer Space" by Nations, 26 November 1957.

[41] Nelson David to Henry T. Snowden, chief, Aviation Division, Department of State, 23 November 1957.

[42] Approved minutes, 75th Meeting of ACC Legal Division, Department of State, 13 January 1958, Agenda Item I, ICAO Matters-Treatment of the Problem of Sovereignty and Associated Legal Privileges and Rights in Regard to the Use of "Outer Space" by Nations.

[43] M. S. McDougal and L. Lipson, "Perspectives for a Law of Space," American Journal of International Law 52, no. 3 (July 1958): 407, cited in R. Cargill Hall, "The International Legal Problems in Space Exploration, An Analytical Review" (master's thesis, California State University at San Jose, June 1966), 3.

[44] Draft recommendation to [Joseph] Sisco, Department of State, subject: United Nations Consideration of Outer Space Control Proposals, 20 November 1958, attached to Loftus Becker to William W. Hancock, transmittal memorandum, 28 November 1958.

[45] Hancock to Becker, memorandum, subject: United States Declaration on Non-Interfering Space Objects, 1 December 1958.

[46] History, Directorate of Plans, Deputy Chief of Staff, Plans and Programs, HQ USAF, vol. 17, 1 July-31 December 1958, 168. (Hereafter History, DCS/Plans and Programs.)

[47] Monroe Leigh to Becker, memorandum, subject: Legal Status of Non-Interfering Objects, 11 December 1958.

[48] Leon Lipson, discussion leader, Chapter III, "Some Problems of the Near Future and Possible Approaches," 5 May 1960, 79, quoted in Joseph M. Goldsen, "International Political Implications of Activities in Outer Space: A Report of a Conference, October 22-23, 1959," R-0362-RC, Santa Monica, Calif., RAND.

[49] Goldsen and Lipson, vi.

[50] Ibid., vi, 5-6.

[51] Ibid., 31-37.

[52] Outline, "Some Elements Requiring Consideration in Formulating a National Policy on Outer Space," 6, attachment to Mansfield D. Sprague, assistant secretary of defense, to secretary of the Air Force et al., memorandum, subject: Proposal for a National Policy on Outer Space, 25 February 1958.

[53] Ibid.

[54] Testimony, Loftus E. Becker, Department of State legal adviser, to Special Senate Committee on Space and Astronautics, 13 May 1958, 18. Attached to Meeker to Monroe Leigh, transmittal letter, 16 May 1958.

[55] Ibid.

[56] Gen Thomas D. White, "Air And Space Are Indivisible," Air Force Magazine, March 1958, 41; and preface to "Missiles and the Race toward Space," The United States Air Force Report on the Ballistic Missile, 1958, 22. General White's continuum statement certainly impacted the delimitation issue. However, the focus of his statement must also have been the effort of the Air Force to obtain or retain the aerospace function as part of the on-going roles and missions discussions taking place within DOD.

[57] Bowen, 185; and History, DCS/Plans and Programs, 166-67.

[58] Staff Study, Air Doctrine Branch, 8 October 1958, 8-10.

[59] Testimony, Gen Thomas D. White, chief of staff, USAF, Hearings before House Committee on Science and Astronautics, Missile Development and Space Sciences, 86th Cong., 1st sess., 73-74 cited in "Future Air Force Space Policy and Objectives," AF/XO study, July 1977, 13.

[60] Hall, "Legal Problems," 15, 136-37.

Chapter 3

Air Force as a Backseat "Driver" in Space Law Debates

By 1956, as a result of the Air Coordinating Committee's (ACC) efforts at the International Civil Aviation Organization (ICAO), the United States had established a position regarding the evolution of outer space law. However, the United States had yet to formulate an overall or general outer space policy. From 1955 to late fall 1957, US foreign policy and its concomitant international actions regarding outer space had focused on disarmament and "space-for-peace." These efforts were driven by the Eisenhower administration's effort to obtain the free passage through space of intelligence-gathering satellites. As described earlier. Air Force efforts had been primarily focused on precluding an international treaty as being premature. As time passed, the US position was nonetheless evolving to a less hardened opposition to formal statements of space policy and international law.

In November 1957, Secretary of State John Foster Dulles wrote Secretary of Defense Neil H. McElroy to encourage direct communication between the Departments of State and Defense (DOD) on space issues. Dulles requested assistance in formulating a US position regarding proposals for inspections of objects to be sent through outer space to ensure that such objects were for exclusively peaceful and scientific purposes. Such cooperation was further encouraged when State Department legal adviser Loftus Becker recommended to DOD general counsel Robert Dechert that the Defense Department establish a task force to study and cooperate with a State Department task force that had been created to deal with space law. Dechert responded, on 15 January 1958, advising Becker that DOD had followed his advice and that Monroe Leigh, assistant general counsel for international affairs, had been assigned to establish the task force and would be DOD's point of contact with State.

In early 1958 the United States focused less on disarmament and more toward obtaining international cooperation for peaceful uses of outer space. This shift in focus was evidenced within the Air Force by an Air University (AU) study regarding the control of outer space. This study, mentioned earlier, diverged from the existing Air Staff position

41

particularly regarding AU's proposal that an international group should codify rules governing the use of outer space. However, the AU study further recommended that any space vehicle on an orbit, trajectory, or unapproved flight plan deemed inimical to the interests of national security should be considered hostile and that appropriate military countermeasures be taken. [1] However, to many Air Force leaders the policy of promoting the "peaceful uses of space" meant a diminished role for Air Force space interests and a threat to the nation's security. [2]

Secretary of Defense
Neil H. McElroy

Internal DOD Strife and Movement
toward a National Outer Space Policy

Despite the Eisenhower administration's 1956 gag order on military comments regarding space, disagreements within DOD began surfacing outside the department by 1958. These disagreements were between the military services and DOD civilians. The disagreements were due in large measure to the fact that the Eisenhower administration's stalking-horse agenda of establishing the principle of freedom of passage for spy satellites in outer space had been created apparently, as discussed above, by DOD civilians and perhaps a selected few in the uniformed military services. These officials had not shared this information with most of the uniformed military. As a result, when the House Select Committee on Astronautics and Space Exploration raised the issue in 1958 of how to deal with Soviet "spy" satellites, Lt Gen Donald L. Putt, Air Force deputy chief of staff for development, testified that he favored "summary destruction" of such satellites. [3] His testimony was directly contradicted by the testimony of Deputy Secretary of Defense Donald Quarles, who shortly thereafter stated, "I can only express the Defense Department's view of it, that, if they did place in orbit a satellite that had such reconnaissance possibilities, we would consider that it was inoffensive in the sense that (they were) in outer space where (they) could do us no harm and we could not object to it." [4] Clearly, General Putt's position was diametrically the opposite of the Eisenhower administration's goal of achieving freedom of passage in outer space particularly for spy satellites. *The fact was that the Eisenhower administration was pursuing a "far more sophisticated, secretive, and complex path than many at the time appreciated" and had no intention of racing the USSR into space. [5] Air Force leaders opposed the Eisenhower administration's prohibition against the deployment of space based weapons and viewed the limitation as "dangerous and self-defeating." [6]

Lt Gen Donald Putt and Col
Carl J. Reber

Following the Sputniks, the US military perceived that it was caught in a dilemma between Eisenhower's space-for-peace policy and its perceived traditional obligation to protect the United States. Hence, in a February 1958 press conference, President Eisenhower assured the nation

---

* Ironically for eight years, beginning in November 1950 when he endorsed an early RAND recommendation of a reconnaissance mission for satellites. Putt had been the most consistent Air Force and Pentagon proponent of such a satellite reconnaissance program.

that DOD would remain in charge of military space projects even if a new space agency was created. [7] In response, the services while publicly expressing acceptance of the space-for-peace policy also supported efforts to establish US control of outer space, at least, until international arrangements guaranteed the commitment of all other nations to the same space-for-peace policy, As Lee Bowen observes:

> In seeking to adjust to the President's somewhat extreme position and their obligations to safeguard the defense of the United States, the military did not criticize the space-for-peace policy but sought rather to determine for themselves how effective international space law was likely to be, how it could curtail their own activities, and how far they should go in presenting a case for military space projects. [8]

By the spring of 1958, because of the continuing disquietude within the military with the space-for-peace policy. Secretary McElroy requested that the National Security Council (NSC) formulate a national policy on outer space to assuage the restiveness of the US armed forces regarding their responsibilities in outer space. After reiterating "support" for the space for-peace policy, the military services, in their March 1958 responses to the NSC, argued against emasculating military space programs. [9] The NSC's efforts to formulate a US policy for outer space moved faster than the Air Force sponsored Project RAND study (which was initially for Air Force eyes only) of the legal implications of the proposed NSC policy. The Air Doctrine Branch, Deputy Chief of Staff (DCS) for Plans and Programs, which had been coordinating on the NSC plan, forwarded the Air Staff position to the Joint Chiefs of Staff (JCS). The JCS adopted the Air Staff position and in turn recommended that the NSC modify its proposal by essentially withholding judgment until further study could be completed. [10] However, on 18 August 1958, President Eisenhower signed NSC 5814/1 entitled "Preliminary US Policy on Space," which described in detail the purpose and principles for US civilian and military space programs.[*] The NSC policy that Eisenhower adopted generally downplayed the role of the military and

---

[*] Specifically, NSC 5814/1 provided that the US continue its IGY experiments, recognize the UN's interest in space, enter into bilateral agreements with other nations to regulate space activities, invite other nations to participate reciprocally in scientific projects, propose projects for multilateral participation, and assist free world nations on their space projects.

emphasized NASA's role in outer space. Air Force leaders were critical of the new NSC policy and its "leaders continued to chafe at what they considered a policy that produced too modest a defense support space program and prevented offensive weapons development altogether." [11]

RAND finally completed its Air Force sponsored study in the spring of 1959. The report helped solidify Air Force doctrine, namely, that the United States avoid committing itself to any position regarding space law. The RAND study was circulated widely within DOD. Substantive intergovernmental discussions relating to space issues continued to the point that NSC's Operations Coordinating Board (OCB)[*] on 18 March 1959 approved an "Operations Plan for Outer Space." The OCB operations plan translated national security policy statements into specific US programs and courses of action, including the following:

> 1. Promote recognition of the right of passage through outer space of any orbiting objects or vehicles not equipped to inflict injury or damage upon the citizens, territories, or property of any State or any property of its citizens.

> 2. Develop a catalogue of the possible legal issues with regard to outer space programs and analyze specific cases with a view to initiating, where necessary, the formulation of definite US legal positions.

> 3. Continue US initiatives in the UN and its Disarmament Commission calling for technical studies of the design of an inspection system that might make it possible to assure that the sending of objects through outer space will be exclusively for peaceful and scientific purposes.

---

[*] The OCB was composed of the under secretary of state (chair), the deputy secretary of defense, director of central intelligence, director of US Information Agency, director of International Cooperation Administration, and the president's assistants for national security affairs and operations coordination. President Eisenhower's executive order created the OCB on 3 September 1953. Reporting to the president through the National Security Council, the OCB was tasked to perform detailed operational planning responsibilities regarding NSC policies, coordination of interdepartmental agency operational plans to carry out NSC policies, and the execution of NSC plans and policies. Further, OCB was authorized to initiate national security policy. For a partial list of OCB objectives see appendix C.

4. Consider bilateral efforts looking toward the design of such a system.

5. Further consider US policy concerning the scope of control and inspection required to assure that outer space could be used only for peaceful purposes, as well as the relationship of any such control arrangements to other aspects of arms agreements. [12]

DOD shared joint responsibility with the State Department and NASA for these actions. When compared with NSC 5814/1, the OCB proposal "indicated a slight change of thinking, at least within the confines of NSC, that meant modification of space-for-peace policy along lines a little more favorable to the military" so that the military space program was no longer to be as small as possible. [13]

Also in March 1959, Franklyn W. Phillips, acting secretary, National Aeronautics and Space Council (NASC), wrote to President Eisenhower supporting a State proposal that an NASC panel be established to study the technical feasibility of proposals on the use of space vehicles not equipped to inflict injury or damage. A few weeks later Phillips wrote to the secretary of defense and requested DOD appointments for an NASC panel to study such space vehicles. In a letter drafted by Benjamin Foreman, DOD's assistant general counsel for international affairs, Secretary Quarles responded to Phillips as follows:

It would appear desirable that the United States avoid making any unilateral policy statement binding only on the United States and which might conceivably limit or hamper its own freedom of action. Thus it is to the advantage of the United States that no legal restrictions on the use of outer space be established for at least a period of time sufficient to allow the United States to gain a fuller understanding of the spatial environment and to ascertain the extent to which other nations may want to use space to the disadvantage of the United States. [14]

In a May 1959 thesis for the Industrial College of the Armed Forces (ICAF) entitled "Astronautical Law," Col Martin Menter* from the Air

---

* Menter was later promoted to brigadier general and continued to remain active in the formulation of space law.

Force JAG corps, asserted that the Roman maxim ex facto oritur jus (the law rises from fact) was an appropriate mode for developing the law of outer space. [15] While he was more receptive than the Air Force generally to the idea of a space convention, Menter's use of the Roman maxim dovetailed with the Air Force's concept of creating outer space law from actual facts or activities, the ad hoc approach, rather than from principles or theories. Colonel Menter's ICAF thesis was subsequently described by Maj Gen Robert W. Manss, The Judge Advocate General of the Air Force, as "one of the first major treatises in this new field of law." [16] Others have described Menter's thesis as being the most comprehensive discourse on the subject of space law up to that time. (See appendix D for a more extensive listing of other conclusions and recommendations from Colonel Menter's thesis.) The passage of time has validated many of Menter's conclusions.

By the summer of 1959, according to an October 1959 RAND report, there was general agreement in the United States regarding three precepts for outer space law. Leon Lipson, author of the RAND report, noted that although the three might be viewed by some as being "negative," these precepts "clarified basic questions of space law" and were therefore "useful achievements." The three principles were

1. An explicit, comprehensive agreement on a detailed code of law for outer space would be premature at this time.

2. The question of the legal status of outer space is not significant now.

3. The definition, in terms of altitude, of the boundary between airspace and outer space is at best a low-priority question. [17]

Pin-on ceremony for Brig Gen Martin Menter. Maj Gen Kuhfeld (left) and Brig Gen Manss (right) do the honors.

These precepts were in accord with the positions taken and advocated by the Air Force.

Even as the space policy was being finalized in 1959, parts of the military remained disgruntled with the Eisenhower administration's space-for-peace policy. In a 16 December 1959 memorandum regarding Air Force space policy to Maj Gen Harold C. Donnelly, assistant DCS for plans and programs, Maj Gen Richard M. Montgomery articulated the military's frustration with being caught between its obligation to protect the United States and complying with Eisenhower's space-for-peace policy. Acknowledging the existence of the space-for-peace policy, Montgomery stated, "the Air Force believes that there is a great potential in space from a military standpoint, and that this potential must be developed." [18]

The United States continued its effort to evolve its space policy that culminated when President Eisenhower signed NSC 5918/1, U.S. Policy on Outer Space, on 26 January 1960. This last policy statement continued to emphasize NASA's role in the US space program. In a 1961 study for NASA, RAND concluded somewhat tentatively but importantly that,

At least provisionally, space flight appears to be considered not inherently subject to exclusive sovereignty of an "under"-lying national state. The threat that air sovereignty would be extended automatically to space flight seems for the present to have receded. Both the US and the SU [Soviet Union] have behaved as though the national air sovereignty which they acknowledge all states to possess did not extend so as to require them to obtain prior consent for geocentric orbital "over"-flights or for deep-space-probe "over"-flights, though the programming of a few shots whose missions might have been considered "delicate" may have owed something to a desire to avoid "over"-flight of certain territories. Official US statements have gradually approached an explicit declaration that outer space is, in general, free. Legal opinion in the US and the SU has on the whole taken the same position, as has that in other countries. [19]

The RAND report continued: "The final victory of the 'freedom of space' should not be taken for granted. In the history of international air law, roughly analogous notions prevailed for a short time among some, perhaps most, of the interested legal scholars, but opposing ideas and military considerations, later fortified by economic interest, carried the day for national air sovereignty." [20]

Except for its yet to come Project West Ford, the Air Force reached the high water mark of its influence on the development of outer space law in 1958. Through its role at the ACC, it clearly had been effective in advocating a go-slow approach and in its efforts to achieve an ad hoc, decentralized generation of the law based on practice. By its actions within the ACC, the Air Force had succeeded in establishing the principle that practice and technology drive the creation of international outer space law as the fundamental thrust of US policy. The RAND report sustained that momentum. Nonetheless, President Eisenhower had obtained his goal of achieving freedom of passage in outer space. Ironically, for all the tension between the Eisenhower administration and the military regarding the president's space-for-peace policy, the Air Force sponsored approach of deriving outer space law through practice and custom had assisted in providing the means by which Eisenhower's freedom of passage principle had been achieved. All were just unhappy that the Soviet launch of Sputniks I and II was the spark that set the events in motion leading to general international acceptance of that principle.

On 11 August 1960 President Eisenhower signed Executive Order 10883, Termination of the Air Coordinating Committee. EO 10883 transferred certain functions of the ACC to the Interagency Group on International Aviation within the Federal Aviation Administration. The demise of the ACC spelled trouble for the Air Force. Once the ACC was gone, the Air Force had no independent vehicle through which to shape outer space law directly, thus Air Force legal activities relating to outer space were confined to DOD. As a result, the Air Force took a more passive stance while DOD and the Joint Staff became more active in influencing policy direction.

Air Force as a Background Player in the Sovereignty Debate

While the US finally had a space policy, discussions evolving from the policy as to its impact on sovereignty and the legality of reconnaissance satellites continued into the 1960s. However, in general during the 1960s, the main participants in the dialogue were from the Office of the Secretary of Defense (OSD). The Air Force role was usually limited to coordination and to meetings within DOD as discussed below. [21]

During this time the United States and Great Britain engaged in substantive discussions regarding outer space law. In August 1961 the Air Force was asked to comment on a British memorandum entitled "Limits in Space and Cognate Questions." The assistant judge advocate general Maj Gen Moody R. Tidwell concurred that it was unwise to attempt to define a line of demarcation where a nation's sovereignty ended. He noted that the focus of concern should be the activity in space rather than the altitude at which it occurred. "Protection of the subjacent state will argue against agreement to any fixed distance as long as equal danger may exist from above such point." Further, the general expressed concern for the definition of peaceful "purposes" and the disassociation of "peaceful" from "military" purposes. He agreed with the caveat included by the British that "nothing shall prevent the use of military personnel or equipment for scientific research or any other peaceful purpose in outer space." Finally, General Tidwell agreed with the position taken by the British that the legality of the passage of reconnaissance satellites in outer space over another state's territory could be premised on the self-defense provisions of Article 51 of the UN Charter.

In preparation for the 16th UN General Assembly in 1961, the Department of State circulated a position paper proposing a US sponsored initiative titled "Advocacy of a Regime of Peace and Law in Outer Space." Essentially, its purpose was to begin UN discussions of various space law issues. Will Carroll, a civilian attorney assigned to the Air Force JAG's International Law Division, represented the Air Force in meetings with Benjamin Foreman, DOD assistant general counsel for international affairs. Foreman had been designated by Cyrus R. Vance, DOD's general counsel, to define DOD's legal concerns in outer space for the former's use in dealing with a recent State Department outer space initiative.

Cyrus R. Vance (center, arms crossed) gets briefing in Vietnam while serving as secretary of defense. Vance had earlier served as general counsel in DOD and played a key role in formulating the Kennedy administration's space policy, especially as it related to international law.

After discussions with Carroll and representatives of JAGs from the other services, Foreman recommended to Vance that he object to any UN discussion of the legality of orbiting space vehicles. [22] The DOD background paper for a planning luncheon regarding the Department of State initiative noted that the Air Force continued to take the position that no agreements concerning the use of outer space should be made until the United States was assured that the agreements were "genuinely reciprocal." Also noted was the fact that the Air Force had expressed a reservation that any agreements affecting satellites should not overcommit the US to furnishing data from such satellites to other nations and should not affect the operation of military satellites. With the Eisenhower administration gone, the Air Force was out to stop any resurrection of the concept of sharing the fruits of aerial reconnaissance as originally embodied in Eisenhower's "open skies" proposal. The Air Force as well as the Joint Staff expressed reservations regarding the Department of State definition for outer space.

> The consequences of adopting such a definition have not as yet been fully explored; and that a rigid definition of outer space should not be attempted prior to a detailed evaluation by all agencies concerned of possible consequences of such a definition to the US and its allies. The proposed definition would establish a space floor which might at some future date be lower than the capabilities of very high flying aircraft. [23]

The DOD position paper recommended that its reservations be pointed out, that DOD and State further study these reservations, and that the US issue a public statement on outer space at the UN. DOD advocated that any formal resolution be deferred.

In a memorandum summarizing his telephone conversation with Richard Gardner (deputy assistant secretary of state for international organization affairs), William P. Bundy (acting assistant secretary of defense for international security affairs) noted that State had agreed to the DOD position regarding the definition of "outer space." Bundy gave DOD clearance on State's proposal with the understanding that State would proceed carefully in negotiations resulting from the resolution. According to a handwritten note by Howard E. Hensleigh (acting DOD assistant general counsel for international affairs), Professor Lipson of RAND had "critical reservations about the [Richard] Gardner approach," that is, having the United States even engage in such discussions. Bundy wrote to Under Secretary of State for Economic Affairs George W. Ball, stating that "we should not define the limits of outer space." Hensleigh provided a copy of the letter to Vance. The Air Force JAG was apprised later that State had decided that efforts to define outer space were premature. However, State requested a briefing from DOD on the "technical developments bearing on the definition of outer space."

Subsequently, the State Department announced the language of its resolution regarding outer space; it did not include a definition for outer space. However, State did recommend that the Space Council undertake a review of the question of defining the limits of air and outer space. The Joint Staff represented DOD's uniformed services in this review. [24] At the end of 1961, Adlai E. Stevenson, US ambassador to the United Nations, stated to the General Assembly that a demarcation between air and outer space was "premature." Underlying the discussion regarding a definition for outer space and the concomitant determination of sovereignty was the fact that US satellites had been orbiting over other nations for approximately three years without objection. Along the line of what Eisenhower had much earlier concluded, attorneys within OSD and the services agreed that the "internationalization" of outer space was in the US national interest and that "peaceful purposes" were consistent with self-defense under the UN charter. [25]

In February 1962, the JCS, in a memorandum for the secretary of defense, stated two reasons for their opposition to defining outer space: it was premature and it limited military space operations. In a letter to E. C. Welsh, secretary of the National Aeronautics and Space Council, Cyrus Vance restated that DOD's position remained the setting of a limit on sovereignty was neither necessary nor desired. That spring, Maj Gen John M. Reynolds (USAF), vice director of the Joint Staff, recommended to Foreman, DOD's assistant general counsel, that the DOD position on the limits of air and outer space was that "international agreement on definition of outer space [was] neither necessary nor desirable at this time. Should a finite boundary be forced upon us, 20 miles or less would be least disadvantageous." Foreman passed this on to the NASC, which issued its summary of department and agency positions on the issue, noting that none had recommended immediate action for setting an upper limit for airspace.

The line of demarcation issue then lay dormant for several years. By 1964 the generally accepted US position was that satellites orbiting the earth were in outer space. [26] The efforts to complete passage of the Treaty on Principles Governing the Activities of States in the Exploration and Use of Outer Space, Including the Moon and Other Celestial Bodies (commonly known as the Principles Treaty or the Outer Space Treaty) again raised the demarcation issue in 1967. In May 1967, Leonard Egan, Air Force assistant general counsel for international affairs, submitted recommended changes to a draft State Department position paper that Jerome Silber (Foreman's successor as DOD assistant general counsel for international affairs) had provided him. Egan's proposed amendments reiterated the Air Force position. Additionally, Col Paul E. Worthman (deputy director for plans and policy, Office of Space Systems), in a memorandum to Col George D. Overbey (chief, Policy Coordination Division, Policy Planning Staff, Office of the Assistant Secretary of Defense for International Security Affairs), concluded that making a distinction between civil and military satellite observations opened a Pandora's box. Worthman pointed out that satellite perigees "will probably stay above 60 miles-for the foreseeable future-with aircraft ceilings remaining below 20 miles. The residual 40-mile band of space should not present a pressing problem to anyone." None of the Air Force comments from Worthman or Egan were incorporated in either Col Overbey's or DOD's comments to State. [27]

When asked to comment on the State Department's final draft position paper, neither Charles F. Kent, assistant Air Force general counsel, nor Col Worthman responded. Internal DOD discussions continued on the issues of the utilization of and definition for outer space throughout the summer of 1967 without direct Air Force input. OSD and the Joint Staff continued to represent DOD at State. While State proposed to have the United States encourage an international agreement defining outer space-the Air Force advised DOD to resist State's efforts in this regard; the Defense Department adopted the Air Force position. No formal definition of outer space has ever been established.

The State Department not only had taken over the Air Coordinating Committee's function with respect to defining US policy before international groups like the ICAO and UN but had become dominant among government agencies regarding coordination and creation of policy impacting outer space law. Further, within DOD itself, Secretary of Defense Robert McNamara centralized policy making in the Office of the Secretary of Defense at the expense of the service secretaries. Clearly, the Air Force had been relegated to a less influential role and had assumed a reactive posture regarding outer space issues. As discussed below, beginning in 1961, the Air Force JAG unsuccessfully encouraged the Air Force to reverse its reactive role and undertake a proactive posture regarding the development of outer space law.

By the early 1960s, the advent of manned space flights made the creation of an international legal regime regarding many outer space issues other than demarcation imperative. A turning point in the "elaboration" of space law occurred on 20 December 1961 when the 16th General Assembly of the UN unanimously passed Resolution 1721 sponsored by both the United States and the USSR. Resolution 1721 provided the general framework for what would eventually become the 1967 Outer Space Treaty. [28] Part A of the UN resolution stated the UN refusal to recognize any sovereignty in outer space, but nonetheless concluded that outer space was to be free for exploration and use by any and all states in conformity with international law and that outer space was not subject to appropriation by any state.

Even though the United States had become more amenable to, and an actual supporter of concluding international conventions regarding international outer space law, it was not until 1967 that the UN actually adopted the first convention. While the US government (generally State and the White House) became more amenable to the passage of a principles treaty, the Air Force clearly did not encourage or support the passage of such an agreement. Contrary to what they had done with air law, legal scholars did not advocate "freedom of space" but proposed that international law should permit extending sovereignty into outer space and place restrictions on the use of outer space by nation-states. The military establishment, on the other hand, supported sovereignty over and regulated use of airspace under international air law, but opposed sovereignty over and regulation of outer space.

---

[1] Bowen, 185; History, Directorate of Plans, DCS Plans and Programs. HQ USAF, 166-67; and Col Martin B. Schofield, USAF, "Control of Outer Space," Air University Quarterly Review 10, no. 1 (Spring 1958): 101, and attachment, Evaluation Staff, Air War College, "A Position on the International Use of Space," 104.

[2] David N. Spires, Beyond Horizons: A Half-Century of Air Force Space Leadership, rev. ed. (Maxwell AFB, Ala.: Air University Press, 1998), 93.

[3] Jerome H. Silber, Office of the Assistant DOD General Counsel for International Affairs, to chief, Air Force Division, Directorate for Security Review (OASD/PA), memorandum, subject: "Preventive Self-Defense in Space," by Maj George D. Schrader, Case No. 66-3923, 11 May 1966.

[4] House Committee on Astronautics and Space Exploration, Hearings: House Report 11881, testimony of Deputy Secretary of Defense Donald A. Quarles, 85th Cong., 2d sess., 30 April 1958, 1107-8.

[5] Spires, 30.

[6] Ibid., 272.

[7] The birth of a civilian space agency (eventually named the National Aeronautics and Space Administration) was troublesome to the military services. Initially, the services were concerned that such an agency would control even military space operations and later, after Eisenhower put that concern to rest, the services were apprehensive about the budgetary implications of such an agency.

[8] Lee Bowen, "An Air Force History of Space Activities 1945-1959" (Washington, D.C.: USAF Historical Division Liaison Office, August 1964), 185.

[9] Ibid.

[10] History, Directorate of Plans, Deputy Chief of Staff, Plans and Programs, HQ USAF, vol. 17, 1 July-31 December 1958, 167. Hereafter History, DCS/Plans & Programs.

[11] Spires, 80.

[12] Elmer B. Staats, executive officer, Operations Coordinating Board, The Implementation of National Security Policy, presentation, Air War College, Maxwell AFB, Ala., 27 November 1957.

[13] Bowen, 96.

[14] Donald A. Quarles, deputy secretary of defense, to Franklyn W. Phillips, acting secretary, National Aeronautics and Space Council, 15 April 1959.

[15] Col Martin Menter, "Astronautical Law" (thesis, Industrial College of the Armed Forces, Fort Lesley J. McNair, Washington, D.C., May 1959), 68-69.

[16] Maj Gen Robert W. Manss, "Judge Advocates and the Law of Outer Space," JAG Law Review, Special International Law Issue: Symposium on the Law of Outer Space, 7, no. 5 (September-October 1965): 3.

[17] Leon Lipson, discussion leader, Chapter III, "Some Problems of the Near Future and Possible Approaches," 5 May 1960, 79, quoted in Joseph M. Goldsen, "International Political Implications of Activities in Outer Space: A Report of a Conference, October 22-23, 1959," R-362-RC (Santa Monica, Calif.: RAND), 79.

[18] Bowen, 187, cites Montgomery to Donnelly, memorandum, subject: Draft Statement of Air Force Policy with Regard to Space.

[19] Leon Lipson, "Current Problems of Space Control and Cooperation: An Analytical Summary," report for NASA (Santa Monica, Calif.: RAND, 1 July 1961), 2.

[20] Ibid., 2-3.

[21] The reduced profile of the Air Force and the insurgence of DOD officials not only on space issues but in many DOD matters during Secretary of Defense Robert S. McNamara's tenure beginning in 1961 are well-documented. See George M. Watson Jr., The Office of the Secretary of the Air Force, 1947-1965 (Washington, D.C.: Center for Air Force History, 1993), 205-44.

[22] Will H. Carroll, "The Role of the Air Force JAG in the Early Development of the Law of Outer Space," unpublished, n.d., 7. This study is in the personal files of the author.

[23] DOD Planning Luncheon, paper, United States Initiative at the 16th General Assembly, 12 September 1961, 3.

[24] If direct service input was provided, no documentation has surfaced to support such input.

[25] Carroll, 7.

[26] L. Niederlehner, acting DOD general counsel, to president, Naval War College, 30 October 1964. Niederlehner cites Richard N. Gardner, assistant secretary of state for international organization affairs, letter to private attorney, 16 March 1964.

[27] Leonard C. Meeker to Paul Warnke, memorandum, subject: Outer Space Committee on the Study of Outer Space Definition, 19 May 1967; Col George D. Overbey to Jerome Silber, memorandum, subject: Position Papers on Definition of Outer Space, 22 May 1967; Silber to Charles Kent, memorandum, subject: Position Paper on the Utilization of Outer Space, 22 May 1967; Silber to Kent, memorandum, subject: Position Paper on Definition of Outer Space, 23 May 1967; Leonard Egan to Silber,

memorandum, subject: Utilization of Outer Space, 23 May 1967; Col Paul E. Worthman to Overbey, memorandum, subject: Comments on Two Position Papers-Utilization of Outer Space and Definition of Outer Space, 25 May 1967; Overbey to Reis, memorandum, attaching DOD Comments on Position Papers Regarding Definition of Outer Space and Utilization of Outer Space, 26 May 1967; UN Committee on Peaceful Uses of Outer Space, Legal Subcommittee, Position Paper on Definition of Outer Space, 19 June 1967, Geneva, Switzerland; Gen Earle G. Wheeler, chairman Joint Chiefs of Staff, to secretary of defense, subject: Position Paper for Outer Space Legal Subcommittee, 22 June 1967; Wayne Anderson to Overbey and Silber, memorandum, subject: Definition of Outer Space, 14 August 1967; all of the above are attached to Silber to Anderson, memorandum, subject: Definition of Outer Space. 16 August 1967.

28 . J. P. Lorenz, Information Office, United Nations Publications, "Outer Space," Historical Project, 29 October 1968.

Chapter 4

Project West Ford

Even as it was resisting efforts in the early 1960s to formalize international outer space law, the Air Force was involved in Project West Ford, a project that would, inadvertently but directly, impact the development of space law. As proposed, West Ford was designed as an experiment to determine whether a small band of orbiting metal strips could be used as a military network providing a "positive, reliable, and survivable full-time communications capability between commanders and their forces." [1] Project West Ford caused significant debate within the United States and the international scientific community. It raised the legal issue as to whether experiments that potentially could interfere with scientific research should be conducted at the sole discretion of any individual nation-state. [2]

In 1958 the Air Force contracted with the Massachusetts Institute of Technology (MIT) Lincoln Laboratory to study the feasibility of using a widely scattered belt of small metallic strips in orbit around the earth as the primary component of a space-based, worldwide communication system. Lincoln Laboratory, in its Barnstable study, concluded that such a system offered the advantages of physical invulnerability and antijamming protection. [3] Given that insufficient information was available to design the system, the Air Force proposed Project West Ford to fill this void. [4] Initially the Air Force planned to disperse 75 (later 110) pounds of disposable dipoles (thin strips of tin alloy) in outer space thereby creating an orbital belt 30 miles in diameter off which communications signals could be reflected. The Lincoln Laboratory was the Air Force contractor for the project.

The proposal proved controversial particularly with radio and optical astronomers, who were concerned that the belt might interfere with astronomical measurements particularly if the dipoles stayed in orbit beyond their projected one- or two-year life cycles. [5] Astronomers feared that the reflectivity of the belt would harm astronomer's ability to observe outer space. In December 1959, the Space Science Board (SSB) of the National Academy of Sciences appointed an ad hoc committee to examine the consequences of West Ford. In July 1960 the SSB determined that the astronomers had raised legitimate concerns and appointed a special committee to evaluate the project extensively. The SSB concluded that "the first experiment involving 75 pounds of material would not be damaging to astronomy." [6] In November 1960 and again on 3 January 1961, Leo Goldberg, a Harvard University professor of astronomy, wrote to Lloyd V. Berkner, chairman of the National Academy of Sciences Space Science Board and father of the IGY. [7] Professor Goldberg challenged the SSB findings, complaining that the board had failed to evaluate the West Ford proposal sufficiently. Goldberg's main concern was not that the SSB had not recommended that West Ford be stopped, but that the SSB should have more carefully evaluated the Air Force proposal. The SSB discussions and decision regarding West Ford were classified. As a result, Goldberg noted that if the astronomy community had the burden of demonstrating why the project should not be carried out, then the data supporting the project, which had previously not been made available, needed to be circulated among concerned astronomers. [8]

Berkner responded to Goldberg by noting that "mere unsubstantiated expressions of fear of the experiment or its successors" would not suffice and asked that the astronomy community substantiate its concern. Subsequently, Berkner did raise the astronomers' concerns in correspondence with other members of the SSB. Further, the SSB continued to recommend that the technical aspects of the project be made public and offered astronomers the opportunity to observe and measure West Ford. [9] The SSB issued a report in August 1961.

Contained in the SSB report was a letter from Jerome B. Weisner, the special assistant to President Kennedy for science and technology, commending the SSB for its study of Project West Ford. Weisner noted that, as a result of the SSB's actions, the government had established a policy regarding the project. The government concluded that the project would be a one-time shot of short-lived duration and that any further launches of similar experiments would wait until the results of the first effort were fully evaluated, including feedback from astronomers worldwide. In August the Kennedy White House issued the following statement:

> No further launches of orbiting dipoles will be planned until after the results of the West Ford experiment have been analyzed and evaluated. The findings and conclusions of foreign and domestic scientists (including the liaison committee of

astronomers established by the Space Science Board of the National Academy of Sciences) should be carefully considered in such analysis and evaluation.

Any decision to place additional quantities of dipoles in orbit, subsequent to the West Ford experiment, will be contingent upon the results of the analysis and evaluation and the development of necessary safeguards against harmful interference with space activities or with any branch of science.

Optical and radio astronomers throughout the world should be invited to cooperate in the West Ford experiment to ascertain the effects of the experimental belt in both the optical and the radio parts of the spectrum. To assist in such cooperation, they should be given appropriate information on a timely basis. Scientific data derived from the experiment should be made available to the public as promptly as feasible after the launching. [10]

The issuance of this policy statement did not quell the astronomer's dissent.

Later in August, the International Astronomical Union (IAU) passed a resolution appealing "to all governments...launching space experiments which could possibly affect astronautical research to consult with the IAU before undertaking such experiments and to refrain from launching until it is established beyond doubt that no damage will be done to astronautical research." [11] A second IAU resolution thanked the US government for announcing its plans well in advance of launching West Ford and for assuring that future launches would not be undertaken unless sufficient safeguards were obtained against harmful interference with astronomical observations. Nevertheless, the resolution expressed concern that the dipole belt would be long-lived and opposed the experiment until proven otherwise. After the IAU General Assembly meeting, Goldberg again wrote Berkner and informed him of the IAU's actions. He argued that the SSE report failed to indicate that its conclusion that the project would have no adverse affect on science was premised on Project West Ford being short lived. Professor Goldberg noted that subsequent discussions indicated the duration of the experiment depended on the altitude of dispersal. [12]

The Air Force launched a Project West Ford package on 21 October 1961, but the dipoles failed to disperse properly. Subsequent to the abortive launch, the astronomy community played a more active role in the SSB, including having its members placed on the SSB's study group. As a result, in the spring of 1962, the SSB West Ford Study Group recommended that any future dispersion of dipoles occur at an altitude that would ensure that any belt created would be short lived and that information regarding the project would be communicated quickly to the international scientific community, particularly astronomers. [13]

In the meantime, in 1961, the International Council of Scientific Unions (ICSU), to which all major countries belong, tasked its Committee on Space Research (COSPAR) to consider problems of contamination in outer space. The ICSU directed that COSPAR take action regarding West Ford. COSPAR deplored West Ford and demanded prior consultation. In May 1962, COSPAR established the Consultative Group of Potentially Harmful Effects of Space Experiments. This committee, consisting of international scientists, would evaluate and make recommendations regarding proposed space experiments. In the face of such opposition and Soviet Union condemnations at the UN, Ambassador Adlai E. Stevenson announced that

> The U.S. would conduct no more such experiments until the results of this one were fully analyzed, and in any case none without proper scientific safeguards;
>
> The results of the experiment would be disclosed to interested scientists of all nations;
>
> Prior consultations with scientists would precede any further activity of this nature;
>
> Advance notice of the launching of such experiments would be given in accordance with the procedure recommended by the General Assembly. [14]

On 9 May 1963, a second West Ford package was launched and the dipoles successfully dispersed. About eight weeks later, the SSE issued its final report on West Ford concluding that the project had harmed neither optical nor radio astronomy. COSPAR's Consultative Group also issued a report concluding that West Ford had caused no adverse effect on or interference with either optical or radio astronomy. Nevertheless, the consultation provision "hammered out in the course of discussions of

Project West Ford...[was] included in the space [principles] treaty" completed in 1968. [15]

Review of the Air Force plans for Project West Ford reveals no discussion about the impact of the project on international law. Because of Project West Ford and the debate that ensued regarding it, the United States established the policy that the scientific community would be consulted in the future should West Ford be extended. Such consultation with the scientific community was subsequently included in Article IX of the Treaty on Principles Governing the Activities of States in the Exploration and Use of Outer Space (the Principles Treaty). [16] The Air Force never intended nor had any idea that its Project West Ford might impact outer space law. When the consultation provision was included in the Principles Treaty, the Air Force had unintentionally but clearly and directly impacted the development of international outer space law.

---

[1] "Proposed System Package Plan (abbreviated) for the Program, 861; Phase II (West Ford Phase II Program)," revised 1 November 1962, 1.
[2] R. Cargill Hall, "The International Legal Problems in Space Exploration, An Analytical Review" (master's thesis, California State University at San Jose, June 1966), 41-42.
[3] Proposed System Package Plan for the West Ford Phase II Program, n.d., 10. The Barnstable study was conducted during the summer of 1958 for the Army Signal Corps. The final report of the Barnstable group, "A Short Study of Communications Theory Applied to Military Communications Systems," dated 30 October 1958, proposed Project Needles, which eventually became Project West Ford.
[4] Ibid., in its entirety.
[5] Hall, 41. Later in August 1960, even Gen Laurence S. Kuter, commander in chief, North American Air Defense Command (NORAD), complained to JCS about Project West Ford. He questioned whether the belt might inhibit NORAD's detection and tracking systems. In November the JCS reassured General Kuter regarding his concerns.
[6] Leo Goldberg to Lloyd V. Berkner, 3 January 1961.
[7] Col Martin Menter, "Astronautical Law." (thesis, Industrial College of the Armed Forces, Fort Lesley J. McNair, Washington, D.C., May 1959), 22.
[8] Goldberg to Berkner.
[9] Berkner to Goldberg.
[10] White House policy statement, "Project West Ford: United States Policy" attached to letter, Weisner to Berkner, 11 August 1961.
[11] Hall, 42.
[12] Goldberg to Berkner, 30 August 1961.
[13] SSE West Ford Study Group Draft memo 223, rev., 2 March 1962.
[14] Maj Norman Thorpe, "The Process of Space Law Development," International Law Division, USAF, Office of Judge Advocate General, paper delivered at Major Command Judge Advocate Conference, Bolling AFB, D.C., 16 November 1967, 3.

[15] Ibid.
[16] Ibid.; and Thorpe

Chapter 5

Maj Gen Albert M. Kuhfeld and Air Force Leadership of Space Law Development

Before the Project West Ford controversy, the Air Force had assumed a reactive posture regarding the development of the law. However, even as Project West Ford was stirring controversy, the judge advocate general and many in the Air Force judge advocate general (JAG) corps were becoming restive with this approach. Several years before Project West Ford, Col Richard C. Hagan,[*] a member of the Headquarters Air Force JAG staff, advised Maj Gen Reginald C. Harmon,[†] the first judge advocate general of the Air Force, that the Air Force could not wait until events had passed it by before it formulated a legal position regarding space. Colonel Hagan further advised General Harmon that the Air Force should take a leadership role on the issue. [1]

While Hagan and others in Headquarters Air Force JAG were interested in space matters, General Harmon was not particularly thus inclined. [2] He did, however, participate as a panelist in an October 1959 space law symposium sponsored by a Reserve JAG flight held in New York City. The panel included "notable jurists, attorneys at law and members of the United Nations." General Harmon restated the Air Force position, which was contrary to the positions taken by several of the other panelists. Harmon asserted that it would be "foolhardy to rush to establish a code of general space law at this time." He further noted to the effect that "law is evolutionary and that the people of the earth do not yet have sufficient scientific knowledge of the physical nature of space to draft rules for its regulation." The general argued that "rather than establish premature rules which could prove dangerous because their possible effects cannot be foreseen, it would be more logical to consider each problem individually." General Harmon "explained the practical and political difficulties inherent in having the legislatures or other state machinery of individual nations ratify any kind of international code of general space law." [3]

---

[*] Col Hagan, a JAG reservist, was eventually promoted to brigadier general.
[†] General Harmon served as The Judge Advocate General (TJAG) of the Air Force from 8 September 1948 through 30 March 1960.

Colonel Hagan's advice eventually found more fertile ground with General Harmon's successor, Maj Gen Albert M. Kuhfeld, who became the Air Force acting judge advocate general on 1 April 1960. General Kuhfeld was much more interested in space issues than his predecessor and readily perceived a value in the Air Force being active in dealing with the legal issues associated with outer space matters. Aware that the sovereignty in outer space and other aerospace legal issues needed resolution, he advocated that Air Force leaders take a proactive posture in these areas.

General Kuhfeld, as explained below, reasoned that the Air Force would be better served by taking a leading role in settling these issues, rather than having them resolved by others. In a speech to the Association of General Counsels of American Industry in November 1960, he discussed the evolution of international law and its relationship to outer space law. He described the various options for defining the line of demarcation between airspace and outer space. He stated his agreement with UN Secretary General Dag Hammarskjöld's position that outer space should be free from appropriation by any state. General Kuhfeld reiterated, from Col Martin Menter's thesis, the Roman maxim ex facto oritur jus (law arises from fact) as being applicable to outer space law. He restated the Air Force position that had evolved in the 1950s, namely, that "we have yet, I think, too many square pegs and round holes to think of codifying any space law." However, the general recognized that

> as scientific data is acquired, problem areas will lend themselves to solution. As the scientist and attorney agree as to factual sufficiency, the particular problem area may be presented to the representatives of various national governments for resolution into mutually acceptable rules to govern space activities...For example, we now have experienced the development of nose cones that survive destruction by the atmosphere. We should immediately recognize and agree that damage caused to persons or property be redressed by the nation launching the particular space vehicle. [4]

He concluded that outer space law would evolve as law generally had, and that the UN, which was already undertaking efforts to identify legal problems incident to the exploration of outer space, was the appropriate instrument to lead such discussions. General Kuhfeld's briefing was given wide exposure, having been published in the Air Force Information

Policy Letter for Commanders and in the Senate Committee on Aeronautical and Space Science's compilation of selected worldwide space law papers. [5]

As had been the case in the 1950s within the Air Force, the judge advocate general and the secretary's general counsel were the most active regarding evolving space law issues. In February 1961 General Kuhfeld noted that "the Air Force has taken the lead in the exploration and development in aerospace medicine, we likewise now may make a substantial contribution at a most opportune time to the development of the law concerning aerospace activities." Accordingly, General Kuhfeld requested that Air Force chief of staff Gen Thomas D. White approve Air Force sponsorship of an aerospace law symposium. The symposium was to include luminaries from the scientific, legal, and political fields. General Kuhfeld further noted that the American Bar Association (ABA) had accepted the position that current military satellite programs were within the meaning of "peaceful use of outer space." He observed that it would be in the Air Force's interests to expand on the ABA's conclusion regarding satellites. Kuhfeld asserted that using Air Force technical terminology regarding space as the standard terms of art would facilitate resolution of such issues more consistently with US national interests. [6]

In the spring of 1961, General Kuhfeld met and discussed his proposal with Gen Richard M. Montgomery, assistant vice chief of staff.* Colonel Menter accompanied General Kuhfeld to this meeting, which took place about one year after Francis Gary Powers's U-2 was "downed" in the USSR. [7] After General Kuhfeld introduced Colonel Menter to General Montgomery as one of the US's experts in international space law, Montgomery asked Menter if the United States had violated international law by having Powers fly over Soviet territory. When Menter responded in the affirmative, General Montgomery angrily retorted to the effect that the colonel "didn't know what he was talking about." [8] Both Kuhfeld and Menter were taken aback by Montgomery's reaction. The meeting deteriorated further when the subject of General Kuhfeld's proposed space law symposium was raised. General Kuhfeld had made a sales pitch for the symposium as a way of encouraging Air Staff interest in the issue and as a means for protecting US security interests.

---

* As noted earlier, Montgomery had expressed a concern for the dilemma that the services felt they faced as a result of President Eisenhower's space-for-peace/"open skies" policy.

Lt Gen Richard M. Montgomery,
Air Force assistant vice chief of
staff

General Montgomery responded that the Air Force had little if any interest in the formulation of space law. He added almost as an afterthought that if General Kuhfeld wanted to push the issue further, additional staff work needed to be completed regarding the symposium proposal and then the proposal needed to be referred to the Air Force Council. Both General Kuhfeld and Colonel Menter left the meeting dejected. Nevertheless, in August 1961, responsive to Montgomery's suggestion, Menter submitted a briefing for the Air Force Council to General Kuhfeld. Colonel Menter included an expanded version of the symposium proposal, which emphasized the need for Air Force participation in the development of aerospace law. [9]

In a December memorandum to General Montgomery, General Kuhfeld continued to push the symposium and recapped the prior year's activities regarding outer space law. Additionally, Kuhfeld reiterated his belief that the Air Force, relying on its mix of scientists and lawyers, should take the lead on the matter. He informed Montgomery that, since preparing his initial proposed briefing for the Air Force Council, "events have occurred, or are programmed, which appear to be fast drawing to an end the academic nature of many aerospace law problems. The current impetus is to seek solution to these problems." General Kuhfeld listed numerous events that had occurred between April and October 1961 that substantiated his assertions. He argued that, just as the Air Force had sent JAG officers to McGill University for advanced study in international law, it should send officers to study at the incipient Institute of Aerospace Law at the University of Virginia Law School.

Finally, General Kuhfeld described recent relevant actions taken at the UN. These events included the first ever meeting of the Committee on the Peaceful Uses of Outer Space (COPUOS) on 27 November and US sponsorship of a resolution setting forth proposals for an international agreement on outer space activities. The latter proposed a COPUOS study and recommendation for the resolution of related legal problems. Kuhfeld related that the Department of State had asked that the National Aeronautics and Space Council (NASC) assist in defining the line of demarcation between air and outer space. He noted that NASC was already working on the issue. Concerned that the Air Force was not more on top of the issue, General Kuhfeld noted:

> As "aerospace" is the media of Air Force operations, the Air Force has a vital interest in the resolution of this problem. It is not a problem that is answered by the lawbooks, but one that may be resolved at the conference table. Hence, the solution arrived at will depend upon the views presented for consideration by each nation's representatives. While we assume the U.S. position will not be in conflict with Air Force concepts as to the nation's best interests, the Air Force-if it has not already done so-should consider the problem to assure that those who decide have all the factors that it believes should be considered together with its studies recommendations. [10]

He observed that, while science was moving rapidly, nothing yet had been achieved that would cause him to change his position that there need be no line of demarcation drawn between air and outer space. He concluded that, "if the Air Force is going to influence trends in this area, it must take a positive position soon." Finally, General Kuhfeld indicated that Colonel Menter from the USAF JAG was assigned to the Federal Aviation Administration and available to discuss the issues and to assist regarding the symposium. [11]

In a January 1962 memorandum to Maj Gen Cecil H. Childre, assistant deputy chief of staff for plans and programs, General Montgomery responded to Kuhfeld's urgings. [12] Montgomery requested a "staff position" regarding the outer space delimitation issue from plans and programs for presentation to the Air Force Council no later than mid February. Finally, given General Kuhfeld's memorandum indicating a number of activities occurring in regard to outer space and their potential impact on the Air Force, General Montgomery had apparently begun to realize that events were not waiting for the Air Force. In a memorandum to General Childre, Montgomery stated, "I am certainly disturbed by the fact that outside agencies who have no understanding or appreciation of the military operation in space may be setting in concrete, with the help of the Russians, some international law which will really tie the Air Force hands for future operation in space." [13] Clearly, General Montgomery was beginning to shift his initial position that space law was not an issue of concern to the Air Force.

Later that month General Kuhfeld provided General Childre with a detailed working paper on the "pertinent legal considerations relating to what will evolve as the USAF Perspective on a Law of Outer Space." Included in the working paper were his "Ten Precepts,"[*] which he argued needed to be remembered when formulating the Air Force position. He noted that while aerospace law was in its "infancy," it nevertheless would have a direct impact on Air Force roles and missions. He proposed that the Air Force establish a permanent Air Staff working group on aerospace doctrine, which he described as being "the marriage of legal considerations and operational plans and requirements." [14] General Childre referred Kuhfeld's working paper to the Air Staff and the Joint Staff. Because the Joint Staff was already working on the subject of defining sovereignty in outer space, Childre noted that Gen Curtis E. LeMay, Air Force chief of staff, was to be briefed on the Air Force position during the first week of February. Childre informed General Kuhfeld that there was no time for a presentation to the Air Force Council and that the requirement to present such was withdrawn. While agreeing that the matter merited attention, General Childre opposed the permanent working group noting that a nucleus of such a group already existed and that the current arrangement should be continued. He proposed as an alternative an informal working group chaired by a JAG official. Childre designated two members of his staff to serve on the working group. [15]

---

[*] See appendix E.

Gen Curtis E. LeMay, chief of staff of the Air Force, and General Kuhfeld, reviewing documents relating to the Air Force position on outer space law.

The informal working group was created in 1962. While JAG and plans and programs participated and communicated well, other parts of the Air Staff did not. This lack of communication was noted by Col John J. Latella, chief, International Affairs Division, JAG, in an undated memorandum to General Kuhfeld. Colonel Latella opined that the informal structure simply was not working and that a more formal structure was needed to be effective. In response to Latella's complaints and parroting his arguments, Kuhfeld asked Childre in May to reconsider his initial opposition. General Kuhfeld requested that General Childre concur in the establishment of a permanent working group to be chaired by a member of the latter's office. To support his position, Kuhfeld asserted that the Air Force was "continuing to operate…on the same 'catch-as-catch-can' basis as" it had previously. He further argued that "the technical, operational and legal aspects of the Air Force role in outer space have not yet been precisely defined, however, and we are still a long way from a firm statement of policies and procedures." Accordingly, he noted that the standard, routine Air Staff coordination system was inappropriate for handling these issues. Finally, he wrote, "the fast pace

70

of current developments, domestic and international, in the evolution of the Air Force role in the outer space region of the aerospace poses a requirement for the capability to react quickly, effectively and authoritatively, in order that the Air Force position on each item of interest may be determined and represented to the best effect." [16]

In August, General Childre's successor, Maj Gen Horace M. Wade, responded to General Kuhfeld. General Wade noted that the Air Force Council had decided in July 1962 to have the assistant deputy chief of staff for research and technology (AF/RDC) be the "focal point" for all space matters. Wade also noted that that within AF/RDC an office would be established for the specific purpose. He noted that this focal point in AF/RDC would be responsible for only coordination of these efforts but that the functional offices within the Air Staff would retain responsibility for handling space matters. As General Kuhfeld had earlier requested, General Wade established a permanent working group to consider the policy and legal aspects of space doctrine. Among the responsibilities of the permanent working group was the review of interagency position papers on space policy referred to the Air Force. [17]

Brig Gen Richard C. Hagan. While serving on the JAG staff at HQ USAF, he pressed for a more aggressive stance by the Air Force on the development of international law on space issues. He supported the first Air Force space law symposium and personally financed the costs of the conference.

Though no response was ever made to his initial idea for an Air Force sponsored space law symposium, General Kuhfeld had succeeded in helping to create (from the informal structure) a permanent working group to coordinate the Air Force position. Eventually the Air Force JAG did sponsor a space law symposium in July 1964 in Washington, D.C. Brig Gen Hagan, without Air Force financial assistance and at his own personal expense, and with General Kuhfeld's support, pulled together the first Air Force space law symposium. He did the staff work and accomplished at least informally what Generals Kuhfeld and Menter earlier had not been able to achieve. [18]

The metamorphosis of the growing Air Force interest in space law and doctrine continued, eventually leading to the creation of the Space Panel within the Air Force board structure. [19] However, before the creation of the Space Panel, several conventions and treaties were negotiated. A review of the Air Force's participation during the passage of these various international conventions, from the Principles Treaty* to the Moon Treaty,† reveals an Air Force that was content to simply coordinate and not originate. Although the Air Force JAG has had an attorney assigned to space matters since the 1950s, only relatively recent actions within the Air Force particularly the creation of Space Command, the dedication of personnel assets within the Air Staff as "space experts," the biennial Conferences on the Law Relating to National Security Activities in Outer Space, and a more aggressive approach by the JAG regarding space matters, indicate that General Kuhfeld's recommendation for a more active leadership posture may now be coming to fruition.

---

* Treaty on Principles Governing the Activities of States in the Exploration and Use of Outer Space, Including the Moon and Other Celestial Bodies
† Agreement Governing the Activities of States on the Moon and Other Celestial Bodies.

[1] Maj Gen Richard C. Hagan, USAFR, transcript of interview by Colonels David M. Lewis and Ronald J. Rakowsky, US Air Force Oral History Program, November 1987-May 1989, USAF Historical Research Agency, 66. (Hereafter Hagan, "Oral History.")
[2] Ibid., 66-67.
[3] "Space Law Symposium," US Air Force JAG Bulletin 1, no. 5 (November 1959): 38.
[4] Maj Gen Albert M. Kuhfeld, speech, Legal Problems of Space Exploration, to the Association of General Counsel, Litchfield Park, Arizona, 18 November 1960.
[5] "Legal Problems of Space Exploration," Senate Committee on Areonautical and Space Sciences, 87th Congo 1st sess., 22 March 1961, 73-77.
[6] Kuhfeld to White, memorandum; subject: Proposed USAF Aerospace Law Symposium, 24 February 1961.
[7] Contrary to Khrushchev's announcement on 1 May 1960 and the currently continuing public perception that Powers's U-2 had been shot down, the official explanation has always been that the plane was never actually hit. On 31 May 1960, Director of Central Intelligence Allen W. Dunes testified before the Senate Foreign Relations Committee that Powers plane had never been hit by Soviet ground-to-air missile. But Dunes further tested that the CIA had concluded that a flameout or an undetermined mechanical malfunction caused Powers to come down from the U-2's normal operating altitude to a lower altitude where his U-2 was no longer immune from Soviet missiles and planes. The critical point here is that Powers was no longer operating at a safe altitude. At that time, the CIA was not sure what had actually happened to Powers's U-2.

L. Fletcher Prouty, in his book The Secret Team: The CIA and its Allies in Control of the United States and the World (Englewood Cliffs, N.J.: Prentice-Hall, 1973), asserts that a "secret team" deliberately scheduled the Powers's flight for the 1 May date without Eisenhower's prior approval. Prouty contends that the secret team then sabotaged Powers's U-2 by disrupting or ceasing the hydrogen flow to the U-2's engine so that the U-2 would be forced down within the USSR airspace. The United States would thereby be forced to admit that it had been violating Soviet air space, thus disrupting the peace summit that was scheduled shortly thereafter.

The CIA, in its recently published declassified version of the history of the U-2 program, states that Eisenhower approved a mission to be flown no later than 1 May 1960. This history states that a Soviet SA-2 surface-to-air missile (SAM) had "detonated close to and just behind the aircraft and disabled it at 70,500 feet above the Sverdlovsk area" causing the plane to go out of control and spiral to earth. Thus, the CIA history implies that Powers may have been operating at an assigned altitude lower than 72,000 feet, apparently contradicting Dunes' testimony that a mechanical malfunction or other undetermined problem had caused Powers to descend from the U-2's normal operating altitude of 72,000 feet. Gregory W. Pedlow and Donald E. Welzenbach, The CIA and the U-2 Program. 1954-1974 (Langley, Va.:, Center for the Study of Intelligence, Central Intelligence Agency, 1998), 176-77.

CIA project officials at first speculated that Powers had been operating too low because of pilot error or due to a mechanical malfunction. "Powers maintained that he had been flying at the assigned altitude and had been brought down by a near miss of a Soviet SAM." (ibid., 177.) In a recent conversation with this author, Powers's son said his father always disputed the allegation of pilot error and insisted that he had been flying at the altitude at which he had been directed to fly. Had Powers been flying at 72,000 feet he would have been above the effective range of any known Soviet antiaircraft or air defense weapons (ibid., 93). Whether a mechanical malfunction caused Powers to descend from the U-2's normal, safe altitude of 72,000 feet and thus brought him within range of Soviet air defenses or whether he was directed to fly the lower altitude (seemingly implied in CIA history) remains unclear.

Based on information obtained in March 1963 (long after Dulles' testimony) from a US air attaché in Moscow, the CIA learned that indeed the Sverdlovsk SA-2 battery had fired a "three-missile salvo that, in addition to disabling Powers's plane, also scored a direct hit on a Soviet fighter aircraft sent aloft to intercept the U-2." (Ibid.) Since Powers's aircraft was disabled at 70,500 feet, a valid and unanswered question remains as to why was his aircraft operating a critical 1,500 feet below its normal operating altitude at the time it was disabled.

[8] Clearly, Menter was right and Montgomery wrong. Even CIA director Dulles indirectly admitted that the US had violated Soviet airspace by the passage of the U-2 through it, but justified the espionage nature of the flights as being less offensive than other means of intelligence gathering. Further, Dulles justified the U-2 program as part of an effort to prevent a surprise attack on the US, which justification had also been made by President Eisenhower and Secretary of State Christian Herter. Specifically, President Eisenhower in his statement about the downing of Powers's U-2 made as his first point the fact that "no one wants another Pearl Harbor." Brig Gen Martin Menter, USAF, Retired, memorandum for record, subject: Oral Interview, Pentagon, 21 February 1990, and transcript of interview by Cols David M. Lewis and Ronald J. Rakowsky, US Air Force Oral History Program, July 1987-August 1989, 73-74.

[9] Ibid.

[10] Kuhfeld to Gen Richard M. Montgomery, memorandum, subject: Formulation of Air Force Positions in Aerospace Law, 8 December 1961.

[11] Ibid., 7.

[12] Montgomery to Childre, memorandum, subject: Aerospace Law, 4 January 1962. Information copy to the Air Staff, SAFGC, and SAFMS.

[13] Ibid.

[14] Kuhfeld to Childre, memorandum, subject: Aerospace Law, 19 January 1962.

[15] Childre to Kuhfeld" subject: Aerospace Law, 2 February 1962.

[16] Kuhfeld, to Childre, memorandum subject: Air Staff Working Group on Aerospace Doctrine, 18 May 1962.

[17] Maj Gen Horace M. Wade to Kuhfeld, memorandum, subject: Air Staff Working Group on Aerospace Doctrine, 22 August 1962.

[18] "The Legal, Socio-Technological Problems of Space Exploration," United States Air Force JAG Bulletin 6, no. 5, 11; Hagan, "Oral History," 38-41, 62-63, 66-67.

[19] Kuhfeld, briefing paper, Proposed Briefing to Air Force Council on USAF Role in Development of Aerospace Law, undated.

Chapter 6

The 1972 Liability for Damages Convention

As described earlier, the Air Force strongly advocated the ad hoc approach to the development of outer space law. Yet, even when practice or custom had developed to the point that some states pushed for codification of these customs into conventions, the Air Force resisted their passage. The one notable exception was the Agreement on the Rescue of Astronauts, the Return of Astronauts and the Return of Objects Launched into Outer Space (Rescue and Return of Astronauts Treaty). The Air Force was ardently against US approval of the Treaty Banning Nuclear Weapon Tests in the Atmosphere, in Outer Space and Under Water. Likewise, but less vehemently, it opposed the Treaty on Principles Governing the Activities of States in the Exploration and Use of Outer Space, Including the Moon and Other Celestial Bodies (Principles or Outer Space Treaty). The effectiveness of Air Force opposition to such treaties was muted or diminished by its generally reactive posture within the Defense Department in the early 1960s.

In his history of the Air Force JAG office from 1963 to 1965, Will Carroll examines the involvement of the Air Force's International Law Division in discussions regarding draft State Department position papers for the Principles, Liability,* and Rescue and Return Treaties. Carroll's brief description of this review and coordination process essentially confirms the generally reactive posture of the Air Force from 1963 to 1965 to these developing international outer space conventions. [1]

In July 1959 the United Nations' Committee on Peaceful Uses of Space (COPUOS) first recognized the need for a liability convention. [2] By that date there had been 30 space launches. [3] Pressure to resolve the liability issue increased as the number of launches rose. However, little progress was discernable until 1962, when the United States introduced before COPUOS the first formal "proposal," though not in the form of a draft treaty, to deal with the liability issue. By then, the US and USSR had launched or attempted to launch more than 150 space objects. In 1964 when the United States introduced the first actual treaty, the number of

---

* Convention on the International Liability for Damage Caused by Space Objects.

launchings was approaching four hundred-with the majority initiated by the United States. [4] Nonlaunching nations were, by then, particularly restive over the liability issue.

Will Carroll receiving an award for superior performance. Carroll wrote a history of the Air Force JAG office's role in the coordination and review process on the many international space law conventions under negotiation in the late 1950s.

Air Force participation in the internal US negotiations regarding the liability convention began with the development of a US sponsored proposal to study the issue. These internal discussions concluded with the preparation of a final position paper and instructions to the US delegate to the COPUOS negotiations. From 1962 until 1970, the Air Force's role in the process consisted primarily in commenting through the DOD on the various proposed draft agreements, position papers, and delegate instructions. In only a relatively few instances was the Air Force involved in direct discussions with the State Department.

The first apparent Air Force involvement regarding the liability issue occurred in May 1962 when Col John J. Latella and his associate, Will Carroll, provided comments to the Air Force Directorate of Plans on the issue of liability for space vehicle accidents. The operational Air Force had concerns about various liability standards. Colonel Latella noted that if the principle of "absolute liability" (liability not based on fault) was to be accepted, then a limit for the amount of damages should be recognized. Carroll indicated that the US proposal on liability required extensive technical legal analysis. [5]

During the initial formal meeting of the COPUOS Legal Subcommittee regarding the liability issue in June 1962, the US delegation proposed that the UN secretary general establish an advisory group to draft a liability treaty. The treaty would incorporate five principles:

• Nations and international organizations, when launching space vehicles, were internationally liable (liable for claims no matter where the injury occurred).

• Fault need not be proven.

• Claimants were not required to file in local courts before filing an international claim.

• Claims had to be presented in a reasonable time.

• Disputed claims would be settled by the World Court. [6]

None of these principles specifically addressed Colonel Latella's concerns regarding a limit on the amount of damages to be paid by governments.

While the COPUOS Legal Subcommittee's first formal meeting on the liability issue ended in disagreement, international interest in space law remained high. The UN General Assembly passed a resolution in December indicating strong support and concern for the fact that COPUOS had not moved forward regarding space law issues. Work continued slowly on the liability issue during 1963. One year later, and after it had agreed on certain outer space principles, the UN General Assembly requested that the COPUOS Legal Subcommittee promptly draft an international convention regarding liability in conjunction with a convention regarding the rescue and return of astronauts and space vehicles. [7]

In March 1964, during the third session of the subcommittee, the United States introduced the first complete draft liability treaty. This draft contained no formula for determining compensation for damages. A working group was appointed, as the US and Canada had proposed earlier. The working group discussed the limitation of liability issue previously raised by the Air Force. [8] In preparing for the Legal Subcommittee's next meeting, the Air Force studied copies of the State Department's position paper and a draft convention. The position paper recognized the need for some limit on liability but did not recommend an amount. [9] The Legal Subcommittee resumed its third session in October. [10] While there was movement toward a consensus, no agreement was reached. [11]

In August 1965, H. Rowan Gaither Jr. of the State Department's Office of the Legal Advisor, solicited Defense Department comments on a draft position paper and an agreement on outer space liability. Col Marshal E. Sanders of DOD's International Security Affairs Policy Planning Division forwarded the request to the Air Force. [12] Two weeks later Col Earl A. Morgan, chief of the JAG's International Law Division, provided Colonel Sanders with the Air Force comments. The Air Force proposed one substantive change, namely, that a nation be enabled to unilaterally have the convention's provisions apply to claims against it filed by its own nationals. [13] Colonel Sanders accepted the Air Force's proposal, circulated the revised draft within DOD, and provided a copy to Gaither. [14]

Soon thereafter, Colonel Morgan sent Sanders a memorandum stating Air Force concurrence on the recirculated draft position paper subject to two significant changes. The first objected to the term unlawful activities because it might stimulate discussion "which could result in restriction of US activities in outer space," especially Department of Defense research and development programs. The Air Force recognized the importance of avoiding this language. The second proposed change noted the Air Force's objection to the principle of "uniformity of result."[*] The Air Force urged DOD not "to participate in the settlement or payment of any claims based on this concept." Further, Colonel Morgan proposed six changes to the draft agreement. His suggested changes included provisions to clarify certain vague terms or concepts and a provision that courts of a third party nation where damage occurred could adjudicate the claim.

---

[*] Uniformity of result meant that, for like injuries, individuals from nations with different standards of living would be compensated equally based on their relative standard of living.

Morgan's changes represented the joint views of the Air Force JAG and general counsel. [15] Colonel Sanders immediately forwarded DOD's comments to Gaither at State. The DOD comments retained all of the Air Force proposed changes to the position paper and four of the Air Force's six proposed changes to the agreement. (The two Air Force proposed changes to the agreement that were not included were essentially nonsubstantive.) [16] When the Air Force later tried to correct language in the DOD memorandum forwarded to State, Colonel Sanders informed the Air Force that "there was some question as to whether or not State was prepared to receive the further comments from DOD on the draft agreement as the document had been fully staffed and agreed upon last year." [17]

A meeting to determine, among other things, the extent to which State was willing to consider DOD's comments was held in early September 1965 in the State Department's Office of the Legal Advisor. Gaither, Leonard Meeker (State's legal advisor), Walter Sohier and Paul Dembling (the general counsel and deputy general counsel of the National Aeronautics and Space Administration [NASA], respectively), Colonel Sanders (representing DOD), Alfred P. Rubin (Air Force general counsel's office), and Lt Col Walter D. Reed (Air Force JAG office) attended the meeting. Most of the Air Force proposed changes to the position paper and the agreement were adopted. The Air Force concern for how damages were to be determined-the concept of uniformity of result in settling claims-was discussed but left unresolved. The Defense Department proposed applying the law of the nation where the damage or injury occurred. Meeker indicated that State was uncommitted regarding uniformity of result. Also discussed at this meeting was the definition of the word procures as used in the proposed agreement. DOD's representatives proposed a restrictive interpretation for the term while State and NASA favored a looser view. The Air Force desired more restrictive language to reduce potential US liability. [18]

In mid-September Carroll and Colonel Reed, in conjunction with Walter Wilson, a member of the Air Force general counsel's office, reviewed a new State Department request to coordinate immediately on a minor addition to the policy position. The Air Force interposed no objection. [19] Colonel Sanders coordinated the revised position paper and draft agreement within DOD regarding the proposed liability agreement. Comments were requested for the next day. [20] Responding on behalf of the Air Force, Carroll restated the Air Force concern over the ambiguity of procures that it had raised during the earlier meeting with the State Department. Carroll feared that that term might be interpreted to make the United States liable for damages from launches of missiles purchased from American sources. [21] Subsequently, Colonel Sanders informed State that

> the Air Force has expressed some concern, which Al Rubin and I share, over the ambiguous concept of "procures" as used in the definition of "launching state." While we are willing to accede to Mr. Meeker's and Mr. Sohier's desire for the retention of the loose formulation of this concept, we would have preferred a more precise definition of the term "procures" than is given…Under the proposed explanation of the term, the United States could be held responsible where the launch vehicle was sold or furnished by us under economic aid, scientific assistance, or other programs, but in which we did not have any direct or indirect interest, give any direct assistance, or participate in the actual launch. [22]

The State Department, however, did not adopt the Air Force's proposed change at that time (see below). Typically the Air Force faced short deadlines in the process of reviewing and commenting on State proposals relating to the liability convention.

COPUOS met during the summer of 1966, but dealt almost exclusively with the Outer Space (or Principles) Treaty. [23] Even while actively involved in the COPUOS discussions regarding the Principles Treaty, the United States still continued to refine its position regarding the liability issue. After talks with Great Britain, Belgium, Australia, and Canada, the US outer space delegation suggested revising the draft US convention regarding liability. As the US revision was reported to COPUOS, the United States agreed to join Belgium in introducing a new jointly sponsored draft convention at the next COPUOS session. [24]

Herbert Reis of State's Office of the Legal Advisor and a member of the UN delegation advised DOD regarding the language in a new, draft liability agreement proposed by the US in February 1967. [25] Interestingly and ironically, given the Air Force's earlier opposition to the use of the word procures, the term was deleted from the text of the proposed revised agreement because Belgium "has consistently opposed" it as placing too broad a liability on "any party which launches or procures a space launching." (Emphasis in the original.) In effect, based on the very same logic, Belgium, by changing the US position on their issue, had achieved what the Air Force had tried but failed to do.

In March 1967, Charles Leonard Egan, assistant general counsel of the Air Force, provided preliminary Air Force responses to additional coordination regarding the proposed liability convention. He noted that the short time suspense for comments did not permit a full review of the revised convention. [26] Two weeks later, Reis again urgently requested comments on a revised Article II regarding the liability of a "launching state." [27] At a meeting that month, Defense and Air Force attorneys agreed to accept Article II, subject to certain amendments. These amendments sought to preclude the United States from being liable to those who had assumed the risk by being involved in the launchings or were proximate to the launching site so as to observe the launch. [28]

Subsequently, State's Meeker contacted the Belgian delegate to the UN, suggesting that Belgium and the United States introduce a joint convention. The text of the proposed jointly sponsored convention included the new US language to replace the word procures, as well as the DOD proposed amendment, to Article II. [29] The Air Force was provided a copy of Meeker's letter and was asked for its comments; it. had none. [30] That May, Reis's memorandum regarding the progress at the UN and a draft US position paper was circulated within DOD for comment by the services. Representatives of the services and various DOD agencies met in the office of Colonel Sanders to discuss the position paper. Colonel Overbey, Colonel Sanders's replacement, provided the DOD response to Reis. The response noted that the State Department position paper "ably represent[ed] Defense views and interests." Colonel Overbey added that while it agreed that the liability treaty should be the "first order of business" in Geneva, DOD did not want to see the US lose any leverage in obtaining the resolution of its proposals for the assistance and return of astronauts. He stressed this point as a matter of concern since launching nations were interested in taking care of their astronauts while nonlaunching nations were more interested in the liability issue. [31] Progress was made in 1967 by the COPUOS Legal Subcommittee regarding the liability convention. In January 1968 the UN General Assembly called on COPUOS to urgently complete its work on the liability convention. [32] In May 1968, the final US liability convention position paper-to be presented at the COPUOS Legal Subcommittee during its meetings between 3 June and 27 June-was circulated in the Air Force for comment. [33]

Almost a year later, in March 1969, Harry H. Almond Jr., DOD's assistant general counsel for international affairs, wrote to Reis (State's legal advisor) regarding proposed instructions for the US delegates to the consultations on outer space liability to be held from 9 June to 4 July. [34] In May 1969, while preparing for these consultations, Maj Lawrence J. McCarthy, Air Force Plans and Policy Branch (DCS/P&O), solicited comments from the Air Force general counsel. The latter referred Major McCarthy to its June 1968 comments. [35] He reviewed the proposed instructions for the delegates and advised his JCS contact that the instructions had taken into account "almost all areas of Air Force interest." Additionally, he recommended inserting a statement to the effect that the United States opposed any definition of "outer space." Major McCarthy opposed defining the term space objects so as to preclude any indirect definition of outer space. Such definitions, he reasoned, might handicap Air Force research and development activities in space. [36] These Air Force comments were then coordinated through JCS and submitted as their formal position to Colonel Butler in OSD/ISA. [37] Responding to State, Almond noted that DOD considered the terms space objects and outer space to be "sensitive." [38]

In a memorandum regarding the developments during the first week of the Eighth Session of the COPUOS Legal Subcommittee meetings on the liability convention, Almond described various proposals being discussed. He especially noted that the items of primary interest to DOD, the definitional issues, were not raised other than in passing. [39] Moreover, in his report regarding the Eighth Session, Stephen M. Boyd. State Department Office of the Legal Adviser and UN delegate, noted that the session did not discuss either of the definitional issues-procures and outer space-which were of interest to the Air Force. [40]

In March 1970, Reis asked Almond and Colonel Butler for comments regarding the instructions to be given to the US participants for the April consultations on the liability convention. The instructions made no reference to the earlier concerns raised by the Air Force. [41] Major McCarthy circulated the draft instructions within the Air Force [42] and received only minor emendations to the instructions. [43] Reis circulated revised instructions for the consultations including the proposed minor changes sought by the Air Force. However, none of the concerns expressed earlier by the Air Force were raised at the June-July 1970 Geneva Conference on the Outer Space Liability Convention. [44]

On 29 March 1972 the United States signed the Convention on International Liability for Damage Caused by Space Objects. The Senate advised ratification on 6 October 1972 and the president signed the ratified convention on 18 May 1973. These actions culminated the more than 10 years of negotiations within the United States government as well as at the United Nations.

---

[1] Will H. Carroll, "The Role of the Air Force JAG in the Early Development of the Law of Outer Space," unpublished, n.d., 7. This study is in possession of the author.

[2] Carl Q. Christol, The Modem International Law of Outer Space (New York: Pergamon Press, 1982), 60.

[3] Marven L. Whipple, "Atlantic Missile Range/Eastern Test Range Index of Missile Launchings, 1950-1974,"

[4] Ibid.

[5] Will Carroll and Col John J. Latella (AFJAL) to Lt Col John L. Sutton (AFXPD-PY), memorandum, subject: Liability for Space Vehicle Accidents, 21 May 1962.

[6] Christol, 61-62.

[7] Ibid., 62-63.

[8] Ibid., 66; and USUN to Department of State, "Outer Space Liability Convention-Applicable Law-How We Got To Where We Are," Department of State Airgram, 1 April 1971.

[9] US Delegation, United Nations Committee on the Peaceful Uses of Outer Space Legal Subcommittee, Sess. III (Resumed), 5 October 1964: and Liability for Damage Caused by the Launching of Objects into Outer Space, position paper, 18 September 1964.

[10] Christol (68) refers to the 5 October 1964 meeting as the fifth session.

[11] Christol, 68-69.

[12] Col Marshall E. Sanders to Will Carroll (AFJAL) et al., memorandum with attached draft position paper, subject: Outer Space Liability Agreement, 5 August 1965.

[13] Col Earl A. Morgan (AFJAL) to Col Sanders, memorandum, subject: Outer Space Liability Agreement, 19 August 1965.

[14] Col Sanders to H. Rowan Gaither (DOS), draft memorandum with attached DOD Staff Level Comments, subject: Outer Space Liability Agreement, 23 August 1965.

[15] Morgan to Sanders, memorandum, subject: Outer Space Liability Agreement, 26 August 1965.

[16] Sanders to Gaither, memorandum with attached DOD Staff Level Comments, subject: Outer Space Liability Agreement, 27 August 1965.

[17] Lt Col Walter D. Reed (AFJALB) to Charles Kent (SAFGCI), memorandum, subject: Air Force Comments on Draft Liability Agreement, 7 September 1965.

[18] Reed, memorandum for the record, subject: Outer Space Liability Agreement, n.d.

[19] Walter Wilson (SAFGCI), memorandum for the record with attached notes of Col Sanders indicating clearance called to Department of State. subject: Outer Space, 10 September 1965.

[20] Sanders to Reed et al., memorandum, subject: Revised Position Paper and Draft

Agreement Liability for Damage Caused by Launching of Objects into Outer Space, 13 September 1965.

[21] Carroll to Sanders, memorandum, subject: Outer Space Liability Agreement, 14 September 1965.

[22] Sanders to Gaither, memorandum, subject: Outer Space Liability Agreement, 16 September 1965.

[23] Christol, 70.

[24] Herbert K. Reis (L/UNA) to Dwayne Anderson (OSD/ISA) et al., memorandum, subject: Outer Space Liability Convention, 20 February 1967.

[25] Ibid.

[26] Leonard Egan (SAFGC) to Anderson, memorandum, subject: Outer Space Liability Convention, 3 March 1967.

[27] Reis to Sanders et al., memorandum, subject: Space Liability Convention-Revised Article II, 17 March 1967.

[28] Jerome Silber (OSD/GCI) to Egan, et al., memorandum, subject: Space Liability Convention-Revised Article II, 23 March 1967; and Silber to Reis, memorandum, subject: Space Liability Convention-Revised Article II, 24 March 1967.

[29] Leonard C. Meeker (DOS L/A) to Professor Max Litvine, Belgium Mission to UN, 27 March 1967.

[30] Silber to Egan et al., memorandum with handwritten note from Egan, subject: Space Liability Convention-Revised Article II, 31 March 1967.

[31] Col George D. Overbey to Reis, 11 May 1967.

[32] Christol, 72.

[33] Coordination Sheet SAFGC # R-357-S with attached final position paper, subject: Liability for Damage from Space Activities, 28 May 1968.

[34] Harry H. Almond Jr. (OSD/GCI) to Reis, memorandum, subject: Outer Space Consultations-Proposed Instructions for the United States Delegate in Geneva, 10 March 1969.

[35] Handwritten note on copy of position paper (Second Draft), Liability Convention, n.d.

[36] Maj Lawrence J. McCarthy (AFXOO) to special assistant for arms control JCS, Attn: Lt Col John Granger, memorandum, subject: Draft Department of State Position Paper on a Liability Convention (U), n.d.

[37] Granger to Col Butler (OSD/ISA), memorandum, subject: Position Paper on Liability Convention, 23 May 1969.

[38] Almond to Stephen M. Boyd (DOS L/UNA), memorandum with attachment (see note 33), subject: United States Position Paper on the Liability Convention, 26 May 1969.

[39] Almond, memorandum for the record, subject: Eighth Session of the Legal Subcommittee Devoted to a Proposed Space Liability Convention-First Week of Session, 19 June 1969.

[40] Boyd, "Report of the United States Delegation to the Eighth Session of the Legal Subcommittee of the United Nations Committee on the Peaceful Uses of Outer Space," 18 July 1969.

[41] Reis to Col Butler, Almond, et al., memorandum with attached draft. subject: Outer Space Liability Consultations, 5 March 1970.

[42] Ibid., handwritten comments; and Kim Seneker (SAFGC) to Lt Col McCarthy (AFXPD), memorandum, subject: 5 March 1970 draft US Position for the Outer Space Liability Consultations, n.d.

[43] Reis to Anderson, Almond, et al., memorandum, subject: Outer Space Liability Convention Consultations, 23 March 1970.

[44] Almond to Anderson et al., memorandum, subject: Outer Space Liability Convention-Geneva Conference, June-July 1970, 13 July 1970.

Epilogue

The Air Force encouraged the ad hoc approach to the writing of space law. This approach has been the route that the development of that law has generally taken. Most international law conventions relating to outer space that the various nation-states have passed and accepted have simply codified existing customs and practices among nations. This trend has allowed the unfettered development of technology to drive these customs and practices just as the Air Force desired. Project West Ford is a case in point. Because of the technology it incorporated, the Air Force had a direct impact on the development of environmental provisions that eventually became part of international outer space law.

It is highly unlikely that any delimitation or demarcation between airspace and outer space will be internationally recognized until a particular practice or technological device makes such a definition imperative. In the interim, Eisenhower's "open skies" policy providing for the free passage of vehicles in outer space, wherever that is, has become the internationally accepted custom (law). The Soviets, with the launch of Sputnik I and II, firmly established this principle of outer space law, and the United States with its subsequent overflights in outer space further solidified the principle. The extensive number of overflights occurring each day have made the principle a commonly accepted custom or practice.

Initially, certain Air Force representatives viewed spy satellites as a threat and, thus, subject to summary destruction. This position was diametrically opposite that which the Eisenhower administration so dearly sought to achieve. The military services chafed under Eisenhower's space policies in part because they had never been fully advised nor fully comprehended how these policies would eventually contribute to the strengthening as opposed to the weakening of national security.

The early Air Force proponents of the ad hoc approach to development of the law were correct. The writing of international conventions before the practices of nations and the advent of relevant technology existed would have been an unnecessary exercise. No evidence has surfaced that mankind or the national security interests of the United States have been disserved by the ad hoc approach. Further, because of the ad hoc approach, space related technology has flourished under the present legal regime and, when appropriate, has been transferred to the civilian sector.

This may not have occurred if certain officials of the Air Force had not stuck by their beliefs. The Air Force individuals who attended the "skull sessions" of the Air Coordinating Committee were particularly effective in preserving the ad hoc approach. Even when under pressure from the others to capitulate, particularly given the growing international pressure at the United Nations for the codification of space law, Air Force officials stood their ground. By remaining firm, the Air Force kept the Air Coordinating Committee, and accordingly the United States, in accord with the Air Force position supporting the ad hoc approach to the development of the law.

The existence of the ACC provided a forum within which divergent views from varying levels of authority (in particular midlevel officials) from many government agencies could be brought to bear on an issue. At the ACC, representatives of agencies below today's policy decision-making level felt free to speak their minds and to advocate, argue, and discuss current issues. In essence, the ACC provided a forum from which long-term analysis and planning emerged from the "adversarying" of the current issues among agencies and departments. Interdepartmental working groups and coordination typified by the ACC are more rarely used today. Instead coordination, in general, has degenerated to passing paper.

After the demise of the ACC, coordination of various forms of paper (for example, position papers, memoranda, briefing papers, and other staff documents) became the predominant vehicle to obtain interdepartmental input regarding the proposed US position for the various outer space treaties. By replacing face-to-face discussions and the type of dialogue typical of ACC meetings with paper coordination, effective and efficient crystallization of concepts, plans, doctrine, or policy is lost. Given the present irregular use of such interdepartmental adversarying of current issues and the conversion of previously mid and upper-level career positions to policy positions (that is, politically appointed positions) that has taken place over the past 30 years, the by-product of such adversarying, has been negatively affected. That is not to say that those with political agendas should not have input, but only that the political input should be layered upon or be part of the metamorphosis of an analysis that was not initially driven by political concerns. Face-to-face, in-depth brainstorming by those without a political agenda must not become a lost art in government. The intra and interdepartmental coordination of the liability treaty, described in chapter 6 above, typified the sterile paper coordination process particularly when compared to the discussions at the ACC.

While the ad hoc approach generally has allowed the unfettered development of technology to drive what would become accepted practices and customs, two major exceptions to this approach were the bilateral Anti-Ballistic Missile (ABM) and Anti-Satellite (ASAT) Treaties. ASAT truncated development of weapons lethal to spy satellites while the ABM treaty curtailed the development of antimissile technology. Clearly, certain policy considerations underpinning the efforts to achieve ASAT were consistent with Eisenhower's strong desire to have "open skies"-the freedom of passage for spy satellites in outer space so as to preclude a nuclear Pearl Harbor. More recently, development of technology in support of missile defense initiatives has tested the limits of the ABM Treaty.

As the Air Force considers the "operationalization" of outer space as analyzed by Gen Thomas S. Moorman Jr.'s Blue Ribbon Panel and/or the development, implementation, and placement of force projection weapons (beyond force-enhancing "eyes and ears" systems) in outer space, it must revisit the policy issues underlying the Eisenhower administration's efforts to establish the free passage of intelligence-gathering devices in outer space. Reconsidering these issues is critical given that the unrestricted movement of intelligence-gathering devices in outer space exists as a result of commonly accepted custom and practice. Such accepted custom and practice could change rather quickly should nation-states determine that such free passage is inimical to their national interests. Military history has taught us a Newtonian symmetry regarding military weapons/measures; that is, for every weapon/measure, there will be at least an attempted countermeasure or system.

The positioning of force projection weapons in outer space could result in the loss of our force-enhancing eyes and ears in outer space and recession of the freedom of passage in outer space as a principle of international legal custom and practice. Other nation-states might target our force enhancing systems because they might be unable or refuse to differentiate between our force projection and force enhancement assets. Or they might even view the force enhancing assets as hybrids. The proliferation of expensive civilian assets further complicates the issue. These civilian satellites also would likely be at risk since other nations may be unable or unwilling to differentiate between military and nonmilitary assets. However, if analysis determines that there is a reasonable, probable, and predicable threat to this nation's national interest or terrestrial humankind's existence from an extraterrestrial force (meteor or alien driven), then there are indeed strong considerations supporting the development of and positioning of such force-projection weapons in outer space to protect and defend life on this planet. However, if the development and positioning of such force projection weapon systems is intended for the sole purpose of controlling terrestrial nation-states or terrestrial humankind, the answer is far more problematical.

As the United States has already learned with respect to its global positioning assets, once turned over for use to the earth's body politic, such assets are difficult to retrieve for national security purposes. On the other hand, our current technical capabilities make unlikely the development and launch of any unforeseen hostile offensive weapons into outer space by another earth-bound nation-state. Assuming such, should the US initiate an offensive arms race in outer space that would likely place its eyes and ears at risk? Currently, probably not. Given advancement and higher standards of living associated with the use of outer space now afforded all of terrestrial humankind, all of which benefits are premised on the principle of free passage, outer space is perhaps presently best left preserved as all of terrestrial humankind's asset. Finally, by internationalizing the benefits derived from outer space, perhaps the assets generating such benefits can be made inviolate.

Appendix A

Air Staff Reaction to Project RAND Report Dated 28 October 1957*

The United States should not take hasty action to commit itself to a generalization of space control which in the future could limit progress in development and technological research for space travel.

There should be an expansion of the military role in evaluating advantages and disadvantages which will affect policy,

planning, and coordination required for guiding the efforts of future space activities in favorable directions.

Terminology in naming United States satellites should be considered if the possibility of premature ICAO consideration is to be minimized.

Military implication of outer space activities on United States national security should be outlined.

An exhaustive study should be conducted on the legal aspects, with assignment of responsibility to an appropriate Air Staff agency for such a study.

Study groups should examine space era aspects such as (A) The offensive use of space missiles or satellites; (B) Force structure and strategic concepts; (C) The acquisition of effective deterrence; and (D) Establishment of appropriate international agreements.

The United States should show its readiness to negotiate and conclude agreements on specific projects for international cooperation in uses of outer space, such as (A) continuation of the IGY, (B) further exchange of satellite tracking data, and (C) an effort to launch into space a scientific rocket or satellite designed and perhaps financed under international auspices. (Details of such agreements and the sequence in which they should be proposed or concluded must depend on developing space technology, the current political-strategic situation, and other factors.)

---

* Staff Study, Air Doctrine Branch, Air Policy Division, Directorate of Plans, Deputy Chief of Staff for Plans and Programs, 8 October 1958, 8-9. Copy on file at HQ USAF, Pentagon Support Office, Office of Air Force History.

United States policy on research and development on outer space should not at this point be deferred or delayed pending the elaboration of an international agreement on the legal status of outer space or a United States policy on legal aspects.

Space programs should be formulated in scope and in intensity of effort as dictated by (a) military needs and requirements, (b) scientific needs, and (c) commercial needs, where they can be foreseen. It is unwise to insist that military end-uses must be foreseen at the present time in order ultimately to achieve useful military applications.

The United States should publicly welcome and encourage the general idea of international cooperation in scientific and commercial phases of its own space research and development, and should refrain from stressing any predominantly military purposes of space exploration, except as technical advance jeopardizes free world survival.

Appendix B

Conclusions of the Air Doctrine Branch Study 8 October 1958*

The United States should not at this time conclude general agreements on the ownership of outer space, the legal status of outer space, or the sovereignty of outer space.

Pending acquisition of more precise knowledge of the operation and control of space vehicles and the various uses to which outer space may be put (e.g., U.S. defense interest, science, and commerce), the United States should not claim sovereignty over outer space above its territory, including territorial waters, and it should not recognize corresponding claims made by or on behalf of other states.

Similarly, the United States should not claim that outer space is free for the passage of all space vehicles. (Freedom of passage should depend on the nature of the vehicle, its inferred or intended purpose, its technical characteristics, and other factors. It is not necessary to have or to develop a uniform rule for all activities occurring in a given place.)

If pressed for agreement on the 'status' of outer space or the 'boundaries' between air space and outer space, the United States should at this time direct the negotiation or discussion away from such general legalistic questions and toward specific uses, specific functions, and specific characteristics of spacecraft.

Although political-diplomatic negotiations may result, eventually, in placing some kinds of limitations on uses of space, the uncertainties of reaching such agreements and then the uncertainty of their enforcement make it impossible to base technical plans and programs of space control on the anticipated resolutions of these issues.

The United States should show its readiness to negotiate and conclude agreements on specific projects for international cooperation in uses of

---

* Staff Study, Air Doctrine Branch, Air Policy Division, Directorate of Plans, Deputy Chief of Staff for Plans and Programs, 8 October 1958, 9-10. Copy on file at HQ USAF, Pentagon Support Office, Office of Air Force History.

outer space; such as (a) continuation of the IGY, (b) further exchange of satellite tracking data, and (c) an effort to launch into space a scientific rocket or satellite designed and perhaps financed under international auspices. (Details of such agreements and the sequence in which they should be proposed or concluded must depend on developing space technology, the current political-strategic situation. and other factors.)

United States policy on research and development on outer space should not at this point be deferred or delayed pending the elaboration of an international agreement on legal status of outer space or a United States policy on legal aspects.

Space programs should not be formulated in scope and in intensity of effort as dictated by (a) military needs and requirements, (b) scientific needs, and (c) commercial needs, where they can be foreseen. It is unwise to insist that military end-uses must be foreseen at the present time in order ultimately to achieve useful military applications.

The United States should publicly welcome and encourage the general idea of international cooperation in scientific and commercial uses of space while reserving its freedom to accept, reject, or modify any particular form of such cooperation.

The United States should give maximum appropriate publicity, directly and indirectly, to the scientific and commercial phases of its own space research and development, and should refrain from stressing any predominantly military purposes of space exploration, except as technical advance jeopardizes free world survival.

Appendix C

Excerpts from The Operations Coordinating Board's "Operations Plan for Outer Space" 18 March 1959*

A. <u>Objectives</u>

1. Develop and exploit U.S. outer space capabilities as needed to achieve scientific, military, and political purposes, and to establish the U.S. as a recognized leader in this field.

2. As consistent with U.S. security, achieve international cooperation in the uses of and activities related to outer space for peaceful purposes and with selected allies for military purposes.

3. As consistent with U.S. security, achieve suitable international agreements relating to the uses of outer space for peaceful purposes that will assure orderly development and regulation of national and international outer space programs.

4. Utilize the potential of outer space to assist in programs of scientific cooperation.

F. <u>International Considerations</u>

19. <u>Establishment of an International Framework for Outer Space Programs</u>

a. International Outer Space Law. In order to be prepared to meet proposals which may be made by other countries and to deal with other practical problems as they may arise, the U.S. should develop a catalogue of the possible legal issues involved in outer space programs and should analyze specific cases with a view to initiating, where it may be necessary, the formulation of definite U.S. legal positions.

---

* Draft Operations Plan for Outer Space dated 18 March 1959, approved by Operations Coordinating Board, 25 March 1959, Bromley Smith, Executive Director.

Appendix D

Conclusions of Colonel Martin Menter's Thesis "Astronautical Law" May 1959*

Recognition in air law of sovereignty of a nation in its superjacent airspace was not a determination of the upward extent of a nation's sovereignty.

While there is an ultimate limit to the upward extent of sovereignty, no presently recommended limits have been accepted or matured into international law.

Neither the finite limits of airspace nor of sovereignty above the earth present justifiable issues, but are matters for settlement by international agreement.

From the point upward that sovereignty ends (whether this is eventually determined), outer space by the natural law should be recognized as a 'res communis omnium' (thing common to all).

Activities in space, rather than the question of sovereignty in outer space, give rise to security problems and will determine a subjacent sovereign's tolerance of a particular satellite.

The international community appears to have accepted the orbiting around the world of space vehicles not equipped to inflict injury or unduly interfere with the normal activities of a subjacent state.

International recognition of and international agreements on activities in space will give rise to the further evolvement of rules of astronautical law.

The acquisition of sufficient necessary scientific data concerning astronautical activity is normally a prerequisite to the preparation of a meaningful international rule of law to govern such activity.

The participation of scientists of different nations in common space projects will result in a more rapid advance in the technology of space exploration, the acquisition of scientific data, and in the development of

---

* Thesis, Col Martin Menter, "Astronautical Law," Industrial College of the Armed Forces, May 1959, 67-69, in possession of General Menter (ret).

law arising out of international agreements premised on the scientific data obtained.

While rules may be not yet formulated to resolve many legal problems in astronautics, there are areas where existing data are sufficient to formulate international agreements on space activities.

As (1) the nature of sovereignty is such that a nation is subject to national limitation only if it joins therein, (2) almost all nations are involved in the orbit of satellites, and (3) international cooperation is essential to the peaceful use of outer space, the United Nations is the appropriate agency to seek concurrence of the international community toward meaningful agreements on the peaceful use of outer space.

Retention of a strong military posture, to include manned military space vehicles, is not inconsistent with the concept of the peaceful use of outer space.

As a result, Colonel Menter recommended that:

The United Nations undertake to determine the areas where international agreements on space activities are feasible and to secure such agreements among the UN members. The following areas are recommended as appropriate for current consideration for international agreement:

To cooperate with the United Nations and member nations for the peaceful exploration of outer space.

To disclaim rights of sovereignty to celestial natural masses with all rights of sovereignty to be exercised as may be determined by the General Assembly under the UN charter.

To refer all international disputes arising out of the use of outer space. that are not otherwise resolved by mutual agreement of the parties, thereto, to the International Courts of Justice, with the decision of such court to be binding; and dispute deemed by such court as nonjusticable to be referred by the Court to the Hague Tribunal, or other UN arbitration panel, with the decision of the Hague Court or other UN panel to be final. except as to such appeal that may be granted to the International Court of Justice.

The creation of a permanent standing UN committee to succeed the current United Nations Ad Hoc Committee on the Peaceful Use of Outer Space when such committee completes its mission and submits its report to the 14th session of the General Assembly. The permanent committee to be charged with the study of space problems on a continuing basis with the view of further assuring peaceful cooperation of the family of nations in outer space activities; further, to evaluate proposals including those for formulation of international rules of astronautical law received from the UNASTRA. The committee to circulate to member nations proposals for agreement on astronautical activities, including proposals for astronautical law. International conferences on astronautical law shall be recommended by the committee to the General Assembly when the scientific data and evaluation of proposals received are believed to warrant such conferences.

For indemnification for damages sustained from satellite activities.

Adopt and announce the position that it has no desire to claim sovereignty over celestial and land bodies to the detriment of any nation, and, within the United Nations invites all member nations to jointly (A) disclaim rights of sovereignty over celestial land bodies and (B) agree that sovereignty over celestial land bodies will be exercised as the UN General Assembly may determine.

Should not enter into any agreement on the use of outer space which may impair its military security.

Undertake a review of existing law to determine appropriate amendments necessary to extend such laws to U. S. personnel, property, and activities in outer space beyond the present jurisdiction of the United States.

Appendix E

"Ten Precepts" General Albert M. Kuhfeld
January 1962*

Formulation of international law must take into consideration the unique physical nature of the aerospace medium, i.e., air and space with no boundary between them.

The Air Force must assume the initiative and leadership on aerospace matters within the Department of Defense.

The Air Force evaluation of boundary formulae should be in terms of their impact on Air Force roles and missions.

International agreements which prohibit overflight of State by aircraft without permission should only apply within the air-space.

Outer space should be declared free for use by all and not subject to national appropriation.

The right of self-defense must also be recognized but must be suitably defined in terms of reasonable measures taken in good faith to protect against a present physical danger.

The term "peaceful use" is not incompatible with any and all military uses.

An agreement on registration of launches and orbits should be entered into.

Property rights of launch States in their space vehicles must be recognized.

The Moon and other celestial bodies are not subject to national appropriation.

---

* Attachment to Maj Gen Albert M. Kuhfeld, Air Force Judge Advocate General, to Maj Gen Cecil H. Childre, Asst Deputy Chief of Staff, Plans & Programs, memorandum, Subj: Aerospace Law, 19 January 1962.

Glossary of Terms

ABA	American Bar Association
ACC	Air Coordinating Committee
AF/RDC	Air Force assistant deputy chief of staff for research and technology
ASIL	American Society of International Law
AU	Air University
COPUOS	Committee on Peaceful Uses of Outer Space
COSPAR	Committee on Space Research
DOS	Department of State
IAU	International Astronomical Union
ICAF	Industrial College of the Armed Forces
ICAO	International Civil Aviation Organization
ICSU	International Council of Scientific Unions
IGY	International Geophysical Year
JAG	judge advocate general
JCS	Joint Chiefs of Staff
MIT	Massachusetts Institute of Technology
NASA	National Aeronautics and Space Administration
NASC	National Aeronautics and Space Council
NSC	National Security Council
OCB	Operations Coordinating Board
OSD	Office of the Secretary of Defense
SSB	Space Science Board
UN	United Nations
USSR	Union of Soviet Socialist Republics

Glossary of Key People

BAKER, James G.
Harvard astronomer and lens designer. Leading designer of high acuity
aerial reconnaissance lenses during World War II. Headed Air Force
intelligence systems panel and TCP committee member urging
development of U-2. Designed lenses for U-2.

BECKER, Loftus
State Department legal advisor who recommended that the US president
publish a proclamation recognizing that reconnaissance satellites were in
accord with international law so long as they did not interfere with
terrestrial activities.

BISSELL, Richard M., Jr.
Head of all Central Intelligence Agency (CIA) reconnaissance programs
from 1954 to 1962. Former MIT economics professor and Marshall Plan
official. Became Director of Central Intelligence (DCI) Allen Dulles'
special assistant for planning and coordination in January 1954 and
received responsibilities for the new U-2 project late 1954. Later headed
first photosatellite project and oversaw development of Oxcart. In 1959
became deputy director of central intelligence (DDCI) for plans while
maintaining reconnaissance projects portfolio. Resigned from CIA
February 1962.

CARROLL, Will H.
Long-term, nearly 40 years, civilian attorney with Air Force JAG who
specialized in international law and was present in LeMay's office shortly
after Sputnik when Air Force officers sought direction as to an Air Force
position. Worked with many of the JAG officers and was himself
involved with outer space law issues for Air Force.

COOPER, John Cobb
McGill University professor of international air and space law and
member of Princeton University Institute for Advanced Study. US
delegate to and "father" of the 1944 Chicago international law convention
on airspace law, prodigious author of publications regarding outer space
law, and strong proponent of international treaty establishing freedom of

passage in outer space.

DeSAUSSURE, Hamilton
Major, USAF, JAG officer and member of Cooper's first graduating class at McGill's Institute for International Air and Space Law. Author of first substantive Air Force response to Cooper's proposed international outer space law convention.

DONOVAN, Allen F.
Aeronautical engineer who helped design P-4Q fighter for Curtiss-Wright Corporation. One of the founders of Cornell Aeronautical Laboratory. Beacon Hill study group member.

DULLES, Allen W.
DCI from 1953 to 1961. Initially reluctant to support CIA involvement in aerial reconnaissance, which he viewed as the military's responsibility but became strong supporter of U-2 program when he learned how much intelligence was being obtained. Dulles' interests were mainly human intelligence (HUMINT) and therefore left much of the management of reconnaissance programs to DDCIs Cabell and Bissell.

DULLES, John Foster
Eisenhower administration secretary of state, 1953-59. Argued that passage of Project Genetrix balloons over national territory had not violated international law because the altitude in which they flew was arguably not airspace but outer space.

FOREMAN, Benjamin
Assistant general counsel for international affairs, Department of Defense (DOD). Active DOD attorney in outer space law issues and in particular the Liability Convention.

GARDNER, Trevor
World War II Manhattan project official and later head of General Tire and Rubber before starting his own research and development firm, Hycon Company, building aerial cameras. Initially special assistant to secretary of the air force and later assistant secretary for research and development during the Eisenhower administration's first term. Shared Eisenhower's concern for surprise attack helping lead to creation of Technological Capabilities Panel (TCP).

HAGAN, Richard C.
Brigadier general, Air Force Reserve. JAG officer who played instrumental role in development of Air Force position on outer space law. Personally bore cost of initial outer space law symposium.

HALEY, Andrew J.
Director and general counsel for American Rocket Society. Ally of Cooper in pushing for international outer space law convention.

HENSLEIGH, Howard E.
DOD assistant general counsel for international affairs. Active DOD attorney in outer space law issues and in particular the Liability Convention.

HOWARD, Daggett
Associate general counsel of the Air Force for international civil aviation affairs and Air Force representative to Air Coordinating Committee (ACC) Legal Division. As Air Force representative was a strong and particularly effective advocate who kept the Legal Division and the ACC in accord with the Air Force position and as a result played a major role in precluding International Civil Aviation Organization (ICAO) consideration of Cooper's proposals. Later served as the first general counsel of the Federal Aviation Administration.

JENKS, C. Wilfred
McGill University Institute of International Air and Space Law associate of Cooper who sought the passage of an international outer space law convention recognizing that a nation-state's sovereignty extended three hundred miles above the earth's surface.

KINSEY, Ronald C.
Secretary of the ACC Legal Division.

KILLIAN, James R., Jr.
MIT President. Head of TCP. Along with Edwin H. Land encouraged Eisenhower's support of U-2 program. Later served on Eisenhower's Board of Consultants Foreign Intelligence Activities (BCFIA), cabinet-level science advisor, chair of science advisory board, and later chair of Foreign Intelligence Advisory Board under President John F. Kennedy.

LAND, Edwin H.
Inventor of polarized filters and instant-film camera (Polaroid). Head of TCP group investigating US intelligence-gathering capabilities. Supported development of high-altitude reconnaissance aircraft under civilian not military control. Also on BCFIA.

LEGHORN, Richard S.
MIT graduate (physics). Member of US Army Air Forces in 1942 working for reconnaissance expert Col George Goddard and later chief of reconnaissance 9th Tactical Air Force. Proponent of pre-D day, strategic intelligence. Recalled to active duty during Korean War later serving in Eisenhower administration disarmament office headed by Harold Stassen.

LEIGH, Monroe
DOD assistant general counsel for international affairs and opponent of Becker. Proposed presidential proclamation regarding the legality of reconnaissance satellites as failing to adequately protect DOD space missions. Opposed the use of the law of the sea as the analogous basis for evolving outer space law. Active in the evaluation of proposals leading to the eventual Liability Convention.

LINDSEY, Richard C.
Major general, USAF, and acting assistant deputy chief of staff for operations who was thrust into the middle of Air Force efforts to stop Cooper's efforts.

LOVETT, Robert A.
World War II assistant secretary of war for air who recommended creation of ACC.

MENTER, Martin
Colonel (later brigadier general), USAF JAG corps. Author of "Astronautical Law" (1959), first major substantive Air Force evaluation of outer space law. Coined the phrase ex facto oritur jus as being applicable to space. "Astronautical Law" was perceived to be one of the first major treatises on outer space law generally. Had "run-in" with Lt Gen Richard Montgomery over legality of U-2 flight.

MONTGOMERY, Richard M.
Lieutenant general, USAF. Air Force assistant vice chief of staff who

resisted JAG attempts to pursue space law issues. Initially refused General Kuhfeld's and Colonel Menter's request for Air Force sponsorship of space law symposiums but later changed his position.

NORTON, Paul W.
Colonel, USAF. Director of Air Force JAG Civil Law Division during the mid-1950s. Signed first substantive Air Force legal position in response to Cooper's efforts.

PERKIN, Richard S.
President Perkin-Elmer Corporation. Close friend of Baker and served on Beacon Hill project. Helped decide which cameras to use on U-2.

POWERS, Francis Gary
Air Force reserve officer and CIA U-2 pilot beginning 1956. Eventually most experienced U-2 pilot with over 27 successful missions over USSR. Pilot of Grand Slam mission initiated 1 May 1960 during which his U-2 was downed over USSR. Traded for Soviet spymaster Rudolf Abel. Cleared of all allegations of misconduct related to 1 May 1960 mission, trial, and captivity. Lockheed test pilot and later light aircraft and helicopter pilot for radio and 1V stations. Died in helicopter crash 1 August 1977.

PUTT, Donald L.
Lieutenant general, USAF. Long-term deputy chief of staff for development. Most consistent proponent of a satellite reconnaissance program among uniformed service officers. Recommended summary destruction of Soviet reconnaissance satellites if they passed over the United States.

QUARLES, Donald A.
Initially Eisenhower's secretary of the Air Force. In November 1956 directed that no military satellite would precede a nonmilitary satellite into orbit. Later, as deputy secretary of defense, issued the gag order precluding military officers from talking about space. Explained the benefits to Eisenhower of the USSR having sent first satellite into orbit since it overflew US and other countries in outer space. Even after Sputnik refused to allow a US military satellite to precede a nonmilitary satellite into outer space.

ROTHSCHILD, Louis S.
Eisenhower administration ACC chairman and undersecretary of commerce.

SHARP, Dudley C.
Eisenhower assistant secretary of the air force for materiel who served as Air Force representative to the ACC. Opposed Cooper's efforts to achieve an outer space law convention. Opposed even the discussion of outer space law issues at the ACC as being premature given that national security concerns had not been fully evaluated. Sharp also proposed that the US should seek ICAO's adoption of this position. Later secretary of the Air Force December 1959 to January 1961.

WHITE, Thomas D.
General, USAF, First chief of staff of the Air Force to use and argue the services' role as an aerospace force by articulating the air-space continuum doctrine and therefore opposed the setting of boundaries between air and outer space.